P9-DDW-485

Managed Chaos

Managed Chaos

The Fragility of the Chinese Miracle

Prem Shankar Jha

www.sagepublications.com
Los Angeles • London • New Delhi • Singapore • Washington DC

First published in 2009 by

SAGE Publications India Pvt Ltd
B-1/I-1 Mohan Cooperative Industrial Area
Mathura Road, New Delhi 110044, India
www.sagepub.in

SAGE Publications Inc
2455 Teller Road
Thousand Oaks, California 91320, USA

SAGE Publications Ltd
1 Oliver's Yard
55 City Road
London EC1Y 1SP, United Kingdom

SAGE Publications Asia-Pacific Pte Ltd
33 Pekin Street
#02-01 Far East Square
Singapore 048763

Published by Vivek Mehra for SAGE Publications India Pvt Ltd, typeset in 10/12 pt Sabon by Star Compugraphics Private Limited, Delhi and printed at Chaman Enterprises, New Delhi.

Library of Congress Cataloging-in-Publication Data Available

ISBN: 978-81-321-0076-8 (HB)

The SAGE Team: Rekha Natrajan, Sejuti Dasgupta, Anju Saxena and Trinankur Banerjee

To Jai and Amaya

Contents

List of Tables

Preface

In a world that is becoming more and more of an open book to its inhabitants, there remains one great exception. It is China. To most of us China remains an enigma, a vast *terra incognita*, that is affecting our lives more and more, in ways we scarcely understand. But we have no clear idea of how or why it is doing so. This is not because China is physically inaccessible. On the contrary, it grants tourist visas liberally, is host to a legion of foreign journalists, and is far more liberal in allowing foreign scholars to conduct research on sensitive subjects than India. A great deal is known about China. Indeed, other than the United States, no country that is not involved in a war receives as much sustained media coverage as China does. But even sustained research and diligent reporting has not resolved the manifest contradictions that confront those who attempt to understand China. For instance China is at one and the same time the most autarchic and the most globally interconnected economy in the world. Its average per capita income has gone up 11 times in the past 30 years, and it has lifted more than 400 million people out of poverty. But this has not prevented a rapid escalation of popular discontent that is venting itself in an increasingly determined opposition to the government. China's growth, of nearly 10 per cent sustained for 30 years, is the highest the world has known. Its bounding exports and rising trade surpluses suggest very high levels of efficiency in manufacture. How, then, is it consuming 2.2 times as much energy and three times as much raw materials as India for every dollar of product? How in short, does inefficiency co-exist with supreme competitiveness?

There are similar paradoxes in its international policies. Why has China devalued its currency, the Yuan, or Renminbi, continuously by keeping it firmly tied to a depreciating US dollar, but firmly rejected an opportunity to devalue it sharply when it had a perfectly legitimate excuse to do so after the Asian financial crash in 1997? Why is it undertaking massive infrastructure projects—building ports, roads and railways, in Myanmar, Bangladesh, Pakistan and

Tibet and investing hugely in Sub-Saharan Africa. Is it to encircle and neuter India in international affairs and establish a zone of influence in Africa, much as the US did in Latin America, the Caribbean and the Pacific between 1896 and the First World War? But if that were so why has China been so restrained in its use of force to settle border disputes with its neighbours? Only three of more than a score of disputes have led to war. In the vast majority of cases China has settled borders peacefully, on the basis of compromise. These seeming contradictions are difficult to explain within a single analytical framework.

This book is an attempt to understand how the Chinese State functions. To do so it widens the scope of enquiry to include the interaction of its economic system with its political system and builds a political economy model of its development. With the aid of that model it attempts to explain the pattern of its past development and to predict, cautiously, the principal challenges that it will face in the coming years. It concludes that China's explosive growth is the product of intense competition between cadres at different levels of its governments to capture economic resources for investment. Investment is therefore driven not by signals from the market, but by political competition and by the desire among cadres to accumulate personal wealth by dispensing licensing powers in various ways. This is the genesis of most of the contradictions described above.

The writing of this book was made possible by the Observer Research Foundation, New Delhi, and by the Fairbank Center for East Asian Research, Harvard University. The Observer Research Foundation gave me a generous grant that met the expenses of my research at Harvard. At the Fairbank Center, I have to thank Professors Roderick MacFarquhar, Merle Goldman, William Kirby and Ron Suleski, for inviting me to be a visiting Fellow and guiding the development of my ideas. In Delhi, I wish to thank Mr R. K. Mishra, Admiral Krishan Nayyar, Maharaj Krishna Rasgotra and Baljit Kapoor for their confidence in me, and for their patience and unfailing support, while I was writing this book.

1

Mixed Feelings

Ever since India became independent, Indians have regarded China with a mixture of admiration, envy and apprehension. In the early years, admiration had predominated, albeit tinged with apprehension. Within days of the founding of the Peoples' Republic on 1 October 1949, Beijing Radio had begun to broadcast the government's intention to 'liberate all Chinese territories, including Xinjiang and Tibet. On 7 October 1950, 40,000 Chinese troops invaded Tibet and claimed that it had liberated it from foreign dominion. Just 12 days later, it sent 30 divisions, more than 300,000 soldiers into North Korea to help the Peoples' Republic repel what it considered to be a UN-backed American invasion of North Korea and avert a possible threat to China. Over the next 3 years, it threw in another 200,000 soldiers into the battle and fought a grand coalition of forces, consisting of 360,000 men, 2,300 guns and mortars, up to 1,000 tanks and self-propelled artillery pieces, and 1,600 aircraft, and brought them to a standstill. The apprehension deepened when China began to lay claim over 49,000 sq. miles of territory in the Himalayas that India regarded as its own, and turned into active animosity, underlined by fear, in 1962, after India's defeat in the Sino-Indian border war.

Mr Vajpayee's visit to Beijing in 1978, as foreign minister of the Janata government, Rajiv Gandhi's visit 10 years later as prime minister, and the signature of the agreement on peace and tranquility in the border regions, during the visit of Prime Minister Narasimha Rao in 1993 restored normal relations. In the 1990s, as China's growth rate skyrocketed and Foreign Direct Investment (FDI) poured in, admiration returned, but now tinged with envy. Today the envy is in retreat. As China's growth rate slowed from a dizzy 12 per cent between 1991 and 1995 to 8 per cent between 1996 and 2000, and as India's growth rate accelerated to 6.5 per cent between 1993–94 and 2002–03, Indian economists began to ask themselves what it would take to equal, if not exceed China's growth rate. Writing in *Frontline* in 2000, Subramaniam Swamy, who has been a lifelong student of China's growth concluded 'Catching up with China' is a worthwhile slogan for India's new millennium, along with a national commitment to grow at 10 per cent a year. Both goals are feasible and attainable, and within India's grasp' (Swamy 2000).

Seven years later, as India completed its fourth year of above 9 per cent growth, Swamy's cautious optimism had been replaced by a bursting self-confidence, especially among India's entrepreneurs. Equalling China's growth rate became an unstated national objective but few, even then, really believed that India could do it. For China's economic slowdown had also ended in 2001, and its economy was powering ahead like a last-minute passenger with a train to catch. From 2003 its growth rate regularly exceeded 10 per cent, a figure India is yet to attain, let alone sustain. The inflow of FDI into China also continued to dwarf the inflow into India. By the published official figures of the two countries, between 1992 and 2003, against an FDI inflow of $467 billion into China, India received a mere $28 billion (Guruswamy 2006).[1]

Several economists have pointed out that the figures for China and India are not really comparable. For instance, in 2000, China received $40.7 billion of FDI while India received a measly $3.2 billion. But adjusting these figures to conform with the International Monetary Fund's (IMF's) definition of FDI brings the Chinese figure down to $20.3 billion and raises the Indian to $8.1 billion (Bajpai and Dasgupta 2004).[2] A proportionate adjustment to the inflows from 1992 till 2003 would therefore bring China's cumulative FDI down to $233 billion and push up India's to $70 billion. In 2006, against China's $69 billion, the FDI that flowed into India added up to $23 billion (*China Statistical Yearbook* 2007 and Government of India's Economic Survey 2007–08). The gap, therefore, remains large.

The most important difference is that China's growth has been concentrated mainly in the manufacturing sector, while India's has been concentrated in the services sector. The first is a more stable base for future growth because it has connected China more securely into the global economy than IT and IT-enabled services have connected India, and because industrial growth generates far more employment in the economy as a whole than growth in the services sector.

The prevailing attitude in India was summed up by Mohan Guruswamy in a paper presented at a conference on China and India held in New Delhi, in December 2006:

In 1992, the first year of its reforms, India's per capita GDP was $331. This grew to $477 in 2001. In the same period the Chinese per capita GDP surged from $360 to $878...In the 1990s China grew at the rate of 9.7% while India grew at 5.9%. Quite clearly far from beginning to catch up, we fell well behind. China's GDP (1995 constant US$) has grown eight fold since 1979 and stood at $1.4 trillion in 2003. Chinese GDP was lower than that of India in absolute terms in 1978 but caught up with India in the very next year. The size of the Chinese economy now is twice that of India's. In 2003 India's GDP stood at a mere $601 billion with a population of 1.03 billion. We seem to be catching up with China on the population front but China's GDP still remains a distant and difficult target. (Guruswamy 2006)

China, he pointed out, produced five times as much steel and six times as much cement as India, generated twice as much electricity as India and had three times as much generating capacity. 'When analysing growth rates, social indicators, industrial production and more' Guruswamy concluded, 'it becomes clear that not only has China left India far behind but these gaps are set to widen in the future...even to come abreast with China by 2050 will be an uphill task for India' (2006).

But not every one shares this belief. In 2004, Goldman Sachs published a now celebrated report, the BRICs report, which predicted that by 2039, if its predictions came true, the combined gross domestic products (GDPs) of Brazil, Russia, India and China would exceed that of the US, Britain, France, Germany, Italy and Japan, whom it dubbed collectively as the G-6. Even more startling was its conclusion that India's growth rate would forge ahead of China's around 2013, and will stay ahead till well beyond the mid-point of the century. The gap in their respective dollar GDPs would narrow more slowly because the yuan, whose real value has been held down for almost a decade by pegging it to a falling dollar, would appreciate more in the near future than the Indian Rupee.

Among those who also do not take China's pre-eminence for granted is Yasheng Huang, one of the most respected of Chinese scholars teaching abroad, who is now at Massachusetts Institute of

Technology (MIT). In an article in Foreign Policy, written as far back as 2003, when the Indian renaissance was only beginning, Huang and a Harvard Business School colleague, Tarun Khanna, observed that while China has recorded a much higher rate of growth for much longer, India's growth could easily turn out to be more sustainable. The main reason is that the regulatory and market institutions needed by a mature capitalist economy are far better developed in India than in China. As a result India's capital markets operate with greater efficiency and transparency than do China's, and although it is not without 'flaws', its legal system is also considerably more advanced.

Huang and Khanna also highlighted one important difference between the Indian and Chinese autarchies. When India opted for centralized planning it did not do so with the intention of supplanting the private sector with the public. Instead it planned, from the very beginning, to create a 'mixed economy' in which the government not only set up state-owned enterprises but also nurtured the development of an indigenous entrepreneurial class. By contrast, between 1949 and 1958 China nationalized the private sector that had existed before the birth of the Peoples' Republic. So in 1978, when it began its experiments with the market economy, it had no private sector left, to speak of. Throughout the period of centralized planning, China developed only state-owned enterprises. Indeed it continued to discourage the development of private enterprises till virtually the end of the 1990s in order to protect the state-owned enterprises from competition. As a result, although, India had not attracted anywhere near the amount of FDI that China had, it had spawned a number of companies that had begun to compete internationally with the best that Europe and the United States had to offer. Moreover, many of these firms were in the most cutting-edge, knowledge-based industries—software giants Infosys and Wipro and pharmaceutical and biotechnology powerhouses like Ranbaxy and Dr Reddy's Laboratories, to name just a few. In 2002, they pointed out, the Forbes 200, an annual ranking of the world's best small companies, included 13 Indian firms but just four from mainland China. 'Can India surpass China?' they therefore concluded, was no longer a silly question (Huang and Khanna 2003).

Despite their closely reasoned arguments, Huang and Khanna's thesis attracted relatively little notice till Goldman Sachs issued a report the following year titled, *Dreaming with Brics: The Path to 2050.*

Apart from predicting that by 2040 the combined domestic products of Brazil, Russia, China and India, measured at market (not purchasing power parity rates of exchange, would exceed that of the G-6) the US, Britain, France, Germany, Italy and Japan—it also predicted that by 2015, India's rate of growth would forge ahead of China's, and would stay ahead till 2050 if not longer (Wilson and Purushothaman 2003).

The Indian business establishment took this part of the BRICs report's cautious and conservative predictions at face value. Some of its members began to believe—even boast—that overtaking China was only a matter of time. In China, the report triggered intense irritation. In an interview given to the *Peoples' Daily*, Beijing, only days before President Hu Jintao visited India in November 2006, Wang Jinzhen, the Secretary General of China Council for the Promotion of International Trade (CCPIT), said, 'To use the analogy of the race between the tortoise and the hare for the competition between China and India is fantastic. Only when the hare naps does the tortoise overtake the hare. China will never "nap" in the process of its economic development'.[3]

In the global re-evaluation that followed 'can the Indian Tortoise overtake the Chinese Hare' became a question on everyone's lips. In 2006, the World Economic Forum's international competitiveness rankings put China 11 places behind India. *The Economist* took the opposite track: In a recent comparative survey of India and China, it pointed out that 'China has higher literacy and better infrastructure. It takes a month to start a business in China, and three in India. China has more savings, less debt and less poverty. If this is a race, India has already been lapped' (*The Economist* 2005).

But only a few weeks later Cait Murphy, the Assistant Managing Editor of *Fortune* rebutted this, saying,

> China's hardware—in the form of bridges, roads, ports and the like—is incomparably better than India's. Anyone who has ever been to both Shanghai and Bombay, the countries' respective commercial capitals, does not need any convincing that Shanghai is the more modern and efficient city. But in important ways, India's economic software is superior. India's banks report about 10 percent non-performing loans; China admits to 20 per cent and the true figure could be double that. India's capital markets work the way they should; China's are a rigged casino. India has more engineers and scientists; its domestic entrepreneurs have made a

bigger mark. And while no one in his right mind wants to go near the creaky, backlogged Indian civil courts, India is a country that does try to govern by the rule of law. China, ultimately, is a country that will break the rule of law whenever the Party feels like it or deems its power to be threatened even if that 'threat' is a few thousand poor peasants and their lawyer. (Murphy 2006)

It is our belief that such comparisons serve little purpose because much of China's and India's growth is taking place on divergent tracks. While China has come close to becoming the global hub of outsourced manufacture, India is becoming the global hub for outsourced service industries. The purpose of this book is not, therefore, to add to the long list of such comparative studies that already exists. Rather, it is to explore the way, the Chinese state actually works, and to understand what propels the growth of its economy. To economists the answer might seem obvious and therefore my pursuit trivial. Doesn't China have the highest rate of saving in the world? Does it not attract by far the largest volume of Foreign Direct Investment ever to have flowed into any developing country? Does it not also have an extraordinarily well-educated population and a focused leadership that has embraced the market in a carefully calibrated manner, and has its growth not benefited virtually every section of the population? Is all this not sufficient to explain its rapid and fairly frictionless growth?

Perhaps, but how then does one explain the rising concern in the country for the restoration of 'social harmony'?

Was the approach of the 2008 Olympics in Beijing the only reason why the Chinese government unleashed a wave of repression on human rights activists whom it had previously tolerated, or is there a deeper failure that underlies the growing use of repression? The answer lies in the fact—obscured in the study of economics by the conversion of 'political economy' into 'economics'—that economic change can never be devoid of political consequences. Each shapes, and is in turn shaped by, the other. The political consequences of the transformation to a market economy, in short to capitalism, need to be anticipated and managed in a way that minimizes conflict in society. For political stability is a necessary precondition for sustained, rapid economic growth. China's nervousness stems from the fact that it has not yet found a way of reconciling the two.

Political stability depends upon social stability which in turn requires a reduction of conflict in society. In the short run this can be achieved through the forcible suppression of dissent. But in the longer run disputes need to be resolved, not repressed. Rapid growth shortens the time period within which social and political adjustments have to be made. Therefore, the more the growth accelerates, the more does it become a political and not merely an economic challenge. The right political decisions, taken at the right time, can sustain, and even accelerate, economic growth. The wrong ones or simple inaction in the face of political challenges can stop it dead in its tracks.

In the end, therefore, this book is simply an attempt to understand China's economic development. Its goal is to develop a better understanding of what is propelling China's extraordinary growth, and to understand the numerous anomalies that surround this growth. Why, for instance, is China's growth so highly polluting? Is it simply an unavoidable outcome of its very high rate of growth? Or is it because China's growth is creating large quantities of avoidable waste? All the data point to the second conclusion. China is consuming between two to three times more of raw materials than any other country, for every dollar of GDP that it produces. But this raises several other questions; first, if its growth is both high and extremely wasteful, how long can it be sustained? And second, if despite the wastefulness of its production process China still manages to undercut all other countries in the international market for consumer goods, then who is paying the cost of the extra raw materials, energy and services being consumed in their manufacture? Finally, if this 'surplus' is being forcibly sequestered from workers and peasants, as several writers have pointed out, what are the mechanisms being used and how long will people continue to accept them?

Now that Indians have decided to treat everything that China has done as a beacon for their endeavours, it is all the more imperative to first understand the economic and social cost of the decisions it has taken before deciding whether a pluralist, democratic society can really afford to go down the same road. Not doing so can land Indians in decisions that are both economically and politically unsustainable. These will, to say the least, lead to enormous waste. They could also strain the fabric of our society beyond its breaking point.

Examples of such unthinking, uninformed emulation are beginning to multiply already. Bangalore's new urban development plan is based explicitly upon developing a single core city with tall, gleaming sky-scrapers, in an overt attempt to emulate Singapore and Shanghai. Mumbai is planning to build not one but six magnetic levitation (Mag-Lev) railway lines over a distance of 200 km. Its lodestar is the 30-km Mag-Lev train from Shanghai Airport to Pudong, on the eastern edge of the city. But in their eagerness to emulate Shanghai, they have not bothered to find out its costs and profitability. Had they done so, they would have learned that the Shanghai Mag-Lev train is a white elephant that will take 167 years to recover its cost!

Finally and most damagingly, India's state governments have thrown caution to the winds and are rushing to establish Chinese style Special Economic Zones (SEZs) to attract FDI into export-oriented manufacturing and service industries. What they may not know is that President Hu Jintao has closed 4,755 of the 7,000 SEZs that the Chinese provincial, prefectural and township governments had created after 1988, because these had become the single most dangerous fuse, lighting the flames of discontent in the Chinese society.

This does not mean that we have nothing to learn from China. But to do so, we must first understand precisely what it has achieved, and at what cost.

2

Conflicting Views on China's Development

China's growth has dazzled the world. But, paradoxically, the shimmer of success that surrounds it has become the principal obstacle to assessing its sustainability for it has prevented the construction of a single, coherent narrative of its economic transformation, explaining both its successes and its failures. Instead, there are at least two narratives (with elements of third interwoven into one of them) that are largely inconsistent. The first is a narrative of relentless, purposeful growth, as a dedicated leadership guides China's transition from a state-owned and centrally planned economy to a privatized and highly competitive market economy. To do this, the leadership has seized the opportunity provided by globalization to turn China into the consumer goods factory of the world. Thus, closely related to the first narrative is a supplementary one of successful integration into the global economy that has overshadowed the dramatic achievements of Japan, South Korea, Taiwan, Malaysia and Thailand, two and three decades earlier. This has made China the current exemplar of the virtues of globalization.

The second, which is of more recent origin, is of an economy trapped halfway in what could easily become a failed transition, suffering from rising income inequalities, growing corruption, an increasingly discontented peasantry and an accumulating backlog of unresolved environmental problems. So far there have been only a handful of attempts to fuse the two narratives into one. There is thus no truly satisfying explanation of why discontent should be rising in an economy that has raised gross domestic product (GDP) by more than 11 times in 30 years and lifted a third of its people out of poverty in less than a quarter of a century.

Electrifying Growth

The first is by far the dominant narrative. If the official estimates of the Chinese National Bureau of Statistics are accepted, in the 28 years since it began its transformation from a closed, centrally planned, socialist economy into an open, market-guided one in 1978, it has achieved an average rate of growth of 9.45 per cent. In the first years of the new millennium, the growth rate has actually climbed a shade higher and, till 2008, was firmly in double digits. Despite doubts about the veracity of these estimates, the official figures continue to be accepted and generally quoted without qualification because of the almost miraculous transformation that has occurred within China and its seismic impact upon the world economy.

In 2002, China's GDP was more than eight times what it had been in 1978. In 2006 after, and partly because of, an 18 per cent upward revision of estimates following an exhaustive economic survey by the National Bureau of Statistics, it was 11 times higher. Its per capita income had risen during the same period from $151 in 1978 to $ 2010. The percentage of its population living in urban areas had risen from 18 to 39 per cent, and a prosperous middle class had come into being. Whereas there was one phone line for every 2,000 persons in 1978, there were 98 fixed or mobile phone lines for every 100 persons in 2006. In 1978, only three out of every 1,000 families owned a television set. In 2006, 960 persons out of every 1,000 families owned one.[1]

The number of long distance calls placed in 1978 was 180 million. In 2002, it was 22 billion. In this period, the circulation of newspapers tripled and passenger transport by various means increased from 2.54 to 16 billion. The number of internet users increased from 160,000 in 1997 to over 250 million in June 2008, surpassing the number in the USA; and from almost nil in 1978 the number of Chinese travelling abroad increased to 16 million in 2002 (Pei 2006: 2–3).

At the other end of the scale, as the World Bank pointed out in its report, *China 2020*, within two decades of the commencement of reform, China had lifted 400 million people out of poverty. This extraordinary growth has catapulted China into becoming the fourth largest economy in the world. No other country, not even Japan, has been able to sustain such a mind-boggling rate of growth for such a long time. And no country has so dramatically improved the quality of life of its people, at least judged by the World Bank's yardstick, in so short a time.

Workshop of the World

When there have been so many gainers and so few losers from the changes since 1978, it is difficult to believe that the political system can be anything but stable. But the prevailing impression has been reinforced by the seismic impact that China has had on the global economic system. China's international trade has grown 41-fold from $20.6 billion in 1978 to $840 billion in 2003. One author has described it in the following terms:

> China has administered a bigger shock to the global economy than that created by the UK and US over the 18th and 19th centuries. In 1979, 'China started with 2.9 per cent of world income and grew on an average 6.6 percentage points faster than the world economy for 26 years. The nearest parallel to China was the growth of the United States over the period 1820–70 during which time the differential was 3.3 percentage points (with a lower starting share)' (The World Bank and the Institute of Policy Studies 2006). During the ten-year period ending 2004, China accounted for 9 per cent of the growth in world exports of goods and services, close to 10.7 per cent share of the US. It accounted for nearly 8 per cent of the world growth in imports during the same period, a share second only to the US. In a short period of time therefore, China has come close to becoming the second biggest growth pole of the world after the US. (Bharati 2006)

In economic terms, the shock that its rise has given to the world has been a benevolent one. For China has smoothly filled the slot, created by globalisation, for an offshore platform for the manufacture of labour intensive goods for the world market. This is the role that the east Asian countries were the first to fill. It accounts both for their exceptionally rapid growth, and their transformation into industrialised economies, exporting mostly manufactured goods, within two decades. China is going down the same path. In the last two decades it has emerged as the fastest growing exporter of manufactured goods and has exerted a downward pressure on their prices in relation to those of other products and services. It has also become the undisputed global centre for the manufacture of consumer goods. Factories located in China make 70 per cent of the world's toys, three-fifths of its bicycles, half its shoes, and one-third of its luggage (Shenkar 2005: 2). Its dominance is no longer confined to these basic consumer goods, for it now manufactures half of the world's microwave ovens, one-third of its television sets, a quarter of its dish washers and one-fifth of its refrigerators; these products represent the fastest growing segment of its exports. Manufacturers in other countries increasingly rely on Chinese components or sub-assemblies to stay competitive. (Shenkar 2005: 3)

In the 1990s, China graduated from producing labour-intensive goods to becoming an integral part of the global production system for a larger and larger variety of sophisticated consumer goods. Nicholas Lardy has captured this as follows:

A substantial portion of the exporting activity of foreign invested firms in China involves the duty free import of parts and components that are then assembled and exported as final goods. The value of these imports and associated exports is recorded separately by the Chinese Customs Administration and is identified as processing imports and processing exports, respectively. This processing trade has grown steadily and by 2005 the value of processed exports had reached $416 billion, accounting for about 55 per cent of total exports. A large fraction of processing trade is undertaken by foreign affiliates, but domestic firms accounted for about one-sixth of processing trade exports. (China Customs Statistics 2005: 14)

This pattern is especially evident in electronic and information technology products. Exports of these products soared from $16 billion in 1995 to $268 billion in 2005. As a share of China's total exports, electronic and information technology products rose from 11 per cent in 1995 to 35 per cent in 2005. Electronic and information technology products are produced in China predominantly by foreign owned firms and predominantly using the processing form of trade. This means, importantly, that the parts and components required to produce the export goods are imported duty free. This has become an important aspect of China's trade with south-east Asian countries. (Lardy 2006)

The slot that China now fills in the global production and marketing system is evident in the pattern of its exports and imports. In 2004, China's exports were valued at $593.3 billion, while its imports amounted to $561.2 billion. It thus enjoyed a trade surplus of $32.1 billion. But while it had a trade surplus with the US of $80.3 billion and with Europe of $39.4 billion, it had a trade deficit with Japan of $20.4 billion, with Taiwan of $70.6 billion, with South Korea of $34.4 billion and with Hong Kong of $17.8 billion. In sum, while it had a trade surplus of $119.7 billion with the high-wage, first-generation industrialized countries of the West, this was more than offset by a trade deficit of $145.2 billion with the relative newcomers like Japan and the east Asian tigers (*China Statistical Yearbook 2005*).[2] What has happened is not hard to deduce: the basic pattern of trans-Pacific trade established in the 1960s and 1970s under the initial impact of globalization has not altered. All that has happened is that, faced with rising labour costs at home, Japan and the east Asian tigers have disaggregated the manufacturing process itself. They continue to manufacture components that can be mass produced or require high levels of technical expertise, but have moved the most labour-intensive portions of the manufacturing process to China. These typically include the sub-assembly and final assembly of components and packaging for shipment to the consumers.

The speed at which this symbiosis is developing can be gauged from the growth and changing composition of trade between China and the ASEAN6 countries (the five original members and Brunei). ASEAN6's exports to China only amounted to $4.5 billion or 2.2 per cent of total ASEAN exports in 1993. In the next 11 years, they expanded nine-fold to $38.6 billion or 7.4 per cent of total ASEAN exports.[3] ASEAN6 imports from China similarly expanded from $4.3 billion or 1.9 per cent of total imports to $45.22 billion or 7.2 per cent over the same period. In short, in just over one decade China's share of ASEAN's total trade more than tripled. And over the same period, the ASEAN share of China's total trade increased by more than half to reach about 7 per cent. This growth resulted from a substantial change in its commodity composition, particularly of ASEAN exports to China. In the early 1990s, primary products, such as wood and wood articles and mineral fuels, made up the bulk of ASEAN's exports to China. A decade later semiconductors and other parts had replaced these and components that are key inputs in China's burgeoning export processing industry, particularly of electronics and information technology products (Lardy 2006).

The fortuitous role that timing and location have played in ensuring the success of China's economic reform and triggering its dazzling growth cannot be overestimated. Had exactly the same reforms been carried out in the 1960s, they would have had only a limited impact upon China's growth. That was still the era of the nation state and of the last gasp of national capitalism. Tariff barriers were still relatively high, quantitative restrictions and other non-tariff barriers were in common use even in the industrialized countries and, most important of all, capital flows between nations were closely regulated. The information technology revolution that has made it possible to coordinate different parts of a single manufacturing process across national boundaries, and is therefore the key ingredient of globalization, was still a decade or more away. Thus, even sweeping economic reforms then would have done no more than achieve China's original aims when it set up the original four export processing zones (EPZs) in the coastal provinces. These were to create a window for the inflow of technology and advanced managerial practices which could percolate into the state-owned enterprises (SOEs), increase productivity and create new job opportunities both in the SOEs and in the EPZs.

But China opened its economy to foreign investment at just the time when capital flows got deregulated and the rush to find cheap labour production platforms gathered momentum (the late 1980s). What is more, by 1992, when Deng Xiaoping's southern tour ended China's ambivalence about the virtues of growth, Japan seemed to have reached the end of its three-decade-long export-led growth and wages had begun to rise sharply in south-east Asia, causing it to lose its glamour as a destination for investment in search of low-wage production platforms and threatening their stranglehold on the consumer goods markets of the high-wage economies of Europe and the USA. The countries of the region had therefore also begun to look for ways to reduce their costs and retain their competitiveness in developed country markets. The rush of foreign direct investment to China that began in the 1990s therefore owed less to any sudden change of policy in China than to the conjunction of circumstances created by the globalization of capitalism.

These huge inflows—between 1992 and 1999 China received 26.3 per cent of all foreign direct investment in the developing countries—and China's soaring exports and foreign exchange reserves have reinforced the impression of stability and well-being in China. No country with such rapid growth and such limitless penetration of the world market and no county with a trillion dollar reserve of foreign exchange can seriously face problems of sustainability. If it does it has ample means to resolve them.

A Trapped Transition?

Till relatively recently, the above narratives reinforced each other to create an extraordinarily optimistic picture of China's future. Scholars drew freely upon the experience of the east and south-east Asian countries in the 1980s and early 1990s, and upon the theoretical frame created for them by Samuel Huntington in his book *The Third Wave*, to conclude that by increasing the scope for private initiative, income and well-being, China's move from a socialist, planned economy to an increasingly privatized market economy would build pressures for democratization and further economic reform. China's political future was therefore exceedingly bright and would be fully assured when this process was completed (Rowen 1996).

In the late 1990s, however, a second, far less optimistic, narrative began to emerge. While China as a whole was flourishing, large segments of its people were not. The iron rice bowl had been smashed and with this had gone the lifelong security of the state sector employees. Work conditions in the new, non-state enterprises were if anything worse than those in the sweat shops of south-east Asian factories (Chan and Senser 1997); urban unemployment had doubled in the second half of the 1990s and continued to climb despite a renewed spurt of growth in the new millennium. Income differentials between urban and rural dwellers were rising. Social benefits to which the Chinese urban workers were entitled by law had been reduced and were often not paid or paid late. The hordes of migrant workers in the towns enjoyed no social security whatsoever and in the rural areas what little health insurance there once was had all but vanished.

Most serious of all is the all-pervasive corruption among the cadres of the Communist Party and the state bureaucracy. This has created a decentralized predatory regime[4] whose depredations are creating a swelling wave of peasant discontent and anger. While corruption had been widespread in the 1980s too, by the mid- to late 1990s it had taken on a more entrenched and institutionalized form. All the evidence from corruption trials and enquiries showed that the sums being taken had become larger and by people higher and higher up in the party and state hierarchy (Wedeman 2004). This has so disturbed the central party leadership that in 2005, President Hu Jintao decided to highlight the unrest instead of minimizing it and abruptly changed the goals of policy from chasing growth to promoting social harmony.

These contrary perceptions have made it exceedingly difficult to construct a coherent account of the political economy of China's move to the market. All in all the optimistic view of China's future held by the economists has prevailed over the pessimistic assessment of the political scientists and sociologists. In 2006, Andrew G. Walder, then at Stanford University, articulated a widely held view abroad that social protest in China did not pose a threat to the regime because it was being voiced by what he called 'politically non-strategic', that is, marginal sections of the population. These included laid-off, and near pension-age workers, migrant workers and peasants. According to him, the politically strategic sections of the population are the 45 million cadres of the Chinese Communist Party who do not hold any government office and the multitudes of gainers from China's rapid development (Walder 2007). High growth has ensured that the gainers far outnumber the losers. Walder concedes, however, that the 45 million cadres who are not government functionaries are, in a sense, a swing vote. But after the brief flurry of desertions from the ranks during the Tiananmen uprising, these have shown little if any sign of restiveness.

The optimistic view, that China will automatically become more democratic as its income level rises, relies upon a number of fictions which are sustained by a succession of false analogies between what is happening in China and what has happened elsewhere in the world. These are of special importance, for they have stood squarely in the way of creating a single model that explains not only its rapid growth but also its wasteful use of resources and the rapid-rise social discontent.

3

Double Digit Growth?

China's growth has acquired an almost mythic quality. The most enduring of the perceptions that surround it is that of 'double digit growth' Although many harbour doubts in private, few observers, and scholars publicly question the official estimate, that of almost 10 per cent growth for 30 years. This is despite the fact that almost half of it comes from sources that cannot easily be identified or accounted for. Between 1978 and 1995, the unexplained component was 44 per cent of the total. This was one and a half times higher than similar estimates for Japan between 1963 and 1990 and more than twice as high as for South Korea. Ten years later, despite a slowing down of the economy in the 1990s and a sharp rise in its use of energy and raw materials per dollar of gross domestic product (GDP), the unexplained portion was still 40 per cent of the growth rate.[1]

This unexplained residual factor is not peculiar to China. It is to be found in all developing countries. It is usually ascribed to 'technology' or technology-cum-management and is larger in fast-growing countries. But it is far larger in China than in any other country that has ever undergone the capitalist transformation and, as Table 3.1 shows, does not disappear when one assumes that both labour and capital in China have enjoyed increasing returns to scale equal to those enjoyed by the east and south-east Asian market economies.

Table 3.1: Unexplained Share of Growth (per cent)

Country/Period	Constant Returns	Increasing Returns
China 1978–95	44	30
Japan 1963–90	30	9
South Korea 1960–93	21	−2

Source: World Bank Staff Estimates, in *China 2020* Annexe One, p. 107.

Table 3.1 shows that the assumption of an increasing return to scale that more or less fully explains Japan and South Korea's high rates of growth, still leaves two-thirds of the residual unexplained in China.

The World Bank therefore suggested two other explanations for the extra growth. The first one arose from the deficiencies of Chinese statistics. The problem was that the 'official consumption and investment deflators used to convert current price into constant price estimates of the GDP have increased much more slowly in China than alternate measures of inflation'. It therefore recalculated the latter using the consumer price index for adjusting the figures for consumption, and the price index for building materials for adjusting investment. This brought down the official estimate of growth from 1.2 to 8.2 per cent, but still only reduced the unexplained residual portion of growth from 2.8 to 1.6 per cent.[2]

A systematic appraisal of China's growth by Angus Maddison made in 1997 at about the same time as the World Bank made its corrections suggested that the growth rate between 1978 and 1995 had been no more than 7.48 per cent, a full 2 per cent below the official estimate. This was challenged on a number of points by Carsten Holz, on the grounds that Maddison's assumptions were too conservative. But Holz too has not ruled out the possibility that China's growth rate is lower than the official estimate. The only ambiguity is, by how much (Holz 2006).

Holz's is among the few carefully reasoned responses to Maddison's revisions. For the most part, liberal economists in the West have contested both Maddison's corrections and the World Bank's downward adjustments, and continue to cite the Chinese official estimates without reservation or caveat.

How Reliable are the Raw Data?

Somewhat surprisingly, none of the three—the World Bank, Maddison and Holz—seriously questions the reliability of the raw data on which the Chinese GDP estimates are based. Instead the entire debate on China's growth rate has wandered down the blind alley of statistical methodology and petered out. The Bank only questions, and adjusts, the inflation data that China uses to convert current into constant price estimates. Maddison does point out that the system of self-reporting would have become progressively more inaccurate even if enterprise managers and local officials had been scrupulously honest, because of the explosive increase in the number of reporting units. In 1978, there were 348,000 enterprises, but in 1996 the number had increased to 7.87 million. Many of the new, non-state enterprises either could not or did not bother to distinguish between current and constant prices.[3] But most of his analysis is confined to recalculating the Chinese official data using more modern statistical methods.[4]

Not once in their 2006 exchanges did either Holz or Maddison refer to the strenuous efforts that the Chinese government is making to check what it terms 'statistical fraud'. In 1997, China's National Bureau of Statistics (NBS) provided detailed evidence of what the media dubbed 'statistical fraud' when it disclosed that it had discovered 60,000 cases of statistical misrepresentation. Fifty-eight per cent of the misrepresentation involved a probably deliberate over- or under-reporting of data that constituted a violation of statistical regulations issued in 1997. There were systematic biases to the misreporting. Statistics for foreign investment, exports and the output of township and village enterprises was regularly over-reported, but data on rural population and salaries were regularly under-reported (most salary earners in the rural areas were cadres in the township and village administrations) (*Guangming Ribao* 1998).[5]

But a still more fundamental weakness of the Chinese system has developed after the period for which Maddison had made his corrections to the official data. This is the pressure that enterprise managers and provincial and local authorities have come under to show that they are fulfilling their targets. Competition between enterprises and provinces leads to some over-reporting even during an economic upswing when targets were being achieved or surpassed, but to a far more serious overestimation during economic downswings when no one wants to be the first to report bad news to his or her superiors. The effect of the politicization of economic statistics has been described by L. Zhang as follows:

> In 1998, the regional governments all produced growth indicators that preserved the (planned) GDP growth level for that year and for that reason there arose the phenomenon of provincial growth rates exceeding the growth rate of the national economy, and the growth of regions and cities exceeding the growth rates of the provinces, and the growth rate of counties and cities exceeding

the growth rates of the regions...and even worse, some regions turned the achievement or non-achievement of growth indicators into a political issue, which caused the statistics bureaus to receive great pressure under which it became difficult to preserve integrity. (Zhang 1999: 7, quoted in Rawski and Xiao 2001)

Two other Chinese authors, Gan and Li, have summed up the problem as follows, 'Whenever the leaders insist on accelerated growth or when accelerated growth becomes the content of evaluation, then the wind of overstatement flourishes' (Gan and Li 1998).

Chinese statistics were not politicized in the early years of reform. Zhang, Gan and Li are of the view that this became widespread when the administrations at all levels of government began to use statistical indicators of performance as a way of evaluating performance. According to Gan and Li, this happened sometime in the mid-1990s. Writing in 1998 they said 'In the past few years because statistical figures have become one of the main items used for evaluating economic outcomes and for grading leaders...Statistical falsification has become universal' (Gan and Li 1998).

China's exhaustive economic survey in 2005, in which the NBS deployed 30,000 field personnel, showed that even provincial governors had been inflating their performance data. The central government had been unwittingly facilitating this by announcing the expected GDP growth well before the provincial governors announced their individual results. In a quick survey of the data submitted by 17 provinces for GDP growth in 2004, a correspondent of the *South China Morning Post* found that not one had reported a growth rate lower than the official national average announced a few weeks earlier by Beijing (Van Der Kamp 2005).

In the current decade, the massaging of growth statistics may actually have increased, for China's growth has become progressively more smooth and uninterrupted. China's GDP grew by 8.9 per cent in 2002, 10.1 per cent in 2003, 9.9 per cent in 2004, 10.2 per cent in 2005 and 10.7 per cent in 2006. The contrast with 1991–95 when the economy was in a similar boom phase is striking, for the growth rate in those years were 9.1 per cent, 14.1 per cent, 13.1 per cent, 12.6 per cent and 9 per cent, respectively.

The smoothness extends to growth within these years too. It was 9.4 per cent in the last quarter of 2004, 9.4 per cent in the first quarter of 2005, 9.5 per cent in the second quarter and 9.4 per cent in the third quarter. Economists based in Hong Kong immediately queried the third quarter figures because there had been a sharp decline in the trade surplus which should have been reflected in the GDP, and because the Purchasing Managers' Index had shown a decline in manufacturing output in the same quarter. This prompted one of them to describe Chinese statistics as a 'fantasy world'. Economists at foreign investment banks have therefore grown used to making their own calculations of GDP to guide their analysis for China. Since 2003, their in-house calculations have recorded China's GDP growth fluctuating substantially, from a high of 12–13 to 9 per cent, a much greater degree of volatility than the official statistics (McGregor 2005).

One of the main purposes of the 2005 census was therefore to get a more precise estimate of the extent to which enterprise and local authorities were exaggerating their claims. It established that in 2004 the sum of the provincial estimates of GDP was 3.9 per cent higher than the estimates based upon the census (Huang 2006a). The NBS had been aware of the inflation of data and had been applying *ad hoc* corrections for several years. The census therefore gave it a more firm base for making the corrections, but still did not eliminate the fundamental weakness of Chinese statistics—the fact that so long as government and state-owned enterprise officials were responsible for collecting the data on performance and so long as they believed that their careers depended upon their performance, they would have to be more than human not to exaggerate their successes and hide their failures.[6]

In January 2005, in an attempt to prevent the competitive overestimation of their growth by the provincial governments, the central government stripped them of the power to issue key economic statistics (Huang 2005). But this only ensured that exaggerated estimates would not get out into the media before the NBS had had a chance to deflate them. It did nothing to reduce the NBS' dependence upon data whose objectivity could not be vouchsafed.[7]

4

'Friction-free' Growth?

A second myth is the relentlessness of China's 30-year spell of growth. If one were to believe the data published with commendable speed every year by the China National Bureau of Statistics, China has never known a recession. Data for the years from 1978 till 2005, given in the next chapter, show a short sharp drop in the growth rate from 10.8 per cent between 1981 and 1988 to 4.2 per cent between 1989 and 1990. They also show a less pronounced but more prolonged dip from 11.3 per cent between 1991 and 1996 to 7.9 per cent between 1997 and 2001. But the first was at least partly the economic fallout of a political crisis. As for the second, one could hardly call an 8 per cent growth rate—something that other countries would die for—a recession. As a result in 1997, when the outliers of a slowing economy appeared on the horizon, most of the world accepted China's claim that it had engineered a 'soft landing' after a long spell of hectic 'hyper-growth'. This became all the more easy to swallow because in the 1980s the industrialized countries and, with them, the international financial institutions had drawn a fine distinction between a 'recession' and a moderation, or slowdown of growth. Accordingly, they redefined recession to mean not only the downward side of a trade cycle but also an absolute decline in the gross domestic product (GDP) in two successive quarters. As a result, the 'deceleration' of the late 1990s has been variously described as a soft landing and a slowdown, but never as a recession.

But the sanctity of this definition is, to say the least, debatable. Not only is it relatively recent but it also reflects the resurgence of neo-classical economics in the 1980s. Friedman considered the term business cycle to be a misnomer because of its unpredictability. Following Friedman, a majority of theoretical economists have sought to delink recession from the trade cycle. But nearly all their theorizing is based on the post-1960s experience of the highly industrialized countries. Its relevance to rapidly developing economies is debatable, for by the yardstick of an absolute decline in growth, even for just two-quarters few, if any, newly industrializing countries have ever suffered a 'recession'. Yet all of them have experienced trade cycles, and these have been particularly wrenching during the early stages of capitalist development when industrializing countries have still to develop the elaborate regulatory framework that the mature economies take for granted.

A refusal to acknowledge that China suffered not just a slowdown but also a severe recession is the most serious obstacle in understanding China's political economy. For without understanding its effects upon society, it is impossible to explain the 60-fold increase in public discontent that took place between 1993 and 2004.[1]

The Recession of 1996–2001

By whatever name one may decide to call it, the onset of the downward phase of the trade cycle is heralded by a variety of indicators, such as a slackening of demand, the piling up of unsold goods, cuts in retail prices, and hence a decline in the price level, and a decline of fixed capital formation. By these yardsticks China did suffer from a recession in the second half of the 1990s.[2]

The most unambiguous proof of recession was an abrupt decline in consumer demand. This was reflected by a sudden shift from high inflation to a prolonged bout of deflation. After rising by 11.6 per cent per year between 1991 and 1996, consumer prices fell in 1998, 1999 and 2002. In the intervening years, there were small increases but in 2003 the consumer price index was still pretty much where it had been in 1997. The dip in ex-factory prices and in the average cost of new investment (investment deflator) also was even more pronounced.

Those who accept the official data ascribe the sudden change to the Asian financial meltdown, which occurred in July 1997. While the Asian crisis did have an effect, it was almost entirely upon exports, which rose by only 0.4 per cent in 1998 after rising by 20 per cent the previous year. But the slowdown in exports was more than offset by an actual decline in imports. This left the trade surplus pretty much unaffected. Indeed, 1997 and 1998 saw healthy trade surpluses of 335 and 360 billion yuan, which were of the same order as the surpluses recorded in all but one of the preceding 4 years. For foreign trade to reduce aggregate domestic demand and therefore push down prices, there has to be a trade deficit. This condition was not fulfilled in 1998 or 1999.

Empirical evidence of recession was overwhelming. Profits in manufacturing enterprises fell almost to zero and one-third of the enterprises reported making losses (OECD 2003). In the first 9 months of 1998, the consumption of electricity showed almost no change from the previous year. This suggests that manufacturing output was not growing by much (Faison 1999b).

The slowdown in the growth of consumer demand was unmistakable. There was a sharp drop in the sale of consumer goods across the board. Sales of automobiles grew by 4 per cent in January to September 1998 against 26 per cent in the same period of 1997 (*International Herald Tribune* 1998). In February 1999, China's Industry Consultation and Development Corporation estimated that the demand for passenger vehicles would rise by 3.9 per cent and for commercial vehicles by 1.5 per cent in 1999. This would give an overall growth in demand of about 2.5 per cent.[3] Air traffic grew by 30 per cent a year in 1994 and 1995. Then growth slumped to 12 per cent in 1996, 7.5 per cent in 1997 and 6.3 per cent in 1998 (Faison 1999a). This forced the government to ask Boeing and Airbus to postpone the delivery of 43 aircraft that were scheduled for delivery in 1999.

Declining demand was only one half of the government's reason for asking for the postponement. The other was a growing profit crunch in buying the airlines. This made the government decide to postpone the purchase of the new aircraft (since cancelling the orders was too expensive) till the airlines had sold or leased out 40 of their existing aircraft (Faison 1999a). The sales of trucks fell by 2.2 per cent in January to September 1998, and that of motorcycles by 22.4 per cent (*Xinhua* 1998). The sales of other consumer durables also flattened out or declined, and producers and wholesalers were left with huge stocks of unsold goods.[4] This led to price deflation for the first time in China's post-reform history. To clear their stocks, manufacturers, wholesalers and retailers resorted to price cutting. So widespread was this trend that in October 1998, the retail price index fell for the first time ever by 0.4 per cent. The decline accelerated in November and by the end of that month, retail prices had fallen by 2.5 per cent (Jianlin 1998). In the first 5 months of 1999, retail prices of consumer goods were 3.2 per cent below the same period of 1998 (*Xinhua* 1999a).

Indirect evidence of the slowdown comes from more and more anxious appeals to the Chinese to spend more. One favoured explanation of the slowdown was that the government's attempt to 'smash the iron rice bowl' had created a hitherto unknown insecurity in Chinese workers, especially after 1997. They were responding to this by saving more than they did before out of their salaries (Reuters 1999). In an effort to spur consumer spending, the government cut interest rates seven times between May 1996 and May 1999. This brought the rate down from 9 per cent to well below 4 per cent (*Xinhua* 1999b). The government also reduced the down payment required for the purchase of automobiles and houses to 20 per cent of the sale price (*Xinhua* 1999b).

The worst hit was the real estate sector, where a sizable bubble had developed on the back of rampant land speculation and unrealistic expectations about continued growth. Shanghai, where 1,000 skyscrapers had been built between 1990 and 1999, and 500 more were scheduled to be completed by 2008, was teetering on the edge of a property collapse. In 1996, the Shanghai government brought down the price of commercial housing twice, a clear sign of flagging demand (Quingliang 2000b). But this had no effect on the market. In 1997, 70 per cent of the new housing constructed failed to find buyers. Not surprisingly, rents for office space fell by 50 per cent in Shanghai, and 40 per cent in Pudong city and were expected to fall further (Lardy 1998: 82). Table 4.1 charts the nationwide growth of the real estate bubble. It also shows that even in this sector, growth had begun to slowdown as early as 1996, that is well before the Asian financial crisis.

Table 4.1: Accumulation of Unsold Commercial Homes (in sq.m of floor space)

Year	Accumulation	Annual Increase	Rate of Increase (%)
1994	32,890,000	–	–
1995	50,310,000	17,420,000	52.96
1996	62,030,000	11,720,000	23.30
1997	71,350,000	9,320,000	15.02

Source: China Industrial and Commercial Time 1998.

Not surprisingly, office rents fell from 40 to 50 per cent in Beijing and in other cities too. There was also a huge mismatch between the housing that was being created and the housing that was needed. In all, 7 million of the 9 million sq.m of unsold property created in 1997 was residential (Ramo 1998) while the millions of migrant workers who had found jobs in Shanghai had nowhere to stay. Other cities in China were not much better off.

A failure to build housing that people could afford and unable to sell what they had built caused provinces and municipalities to run up huge losses. Apart from Shanghai, Guangdong, Zhejiang and Guizhou, all the other 21 provinces and municipalities of China suffered losses as high as 52 per cent of their total investment in the housing sector (Quingliang 2000b).[5] In all, it was estimated that China has 70 million sq.m of vacant housing at the end of 1997 (Ramo 1998: 71).

The recession was also reflected in low or declining capacity utilization in industry and mounting losses for the state-owned enterprises (SOEs). Some of the worst hit industries were automobiles and home appliances. But excess capacity was also evident in the beer industry, in machine tools, chemicals and chemical fibres. According to an industrial census in 1995, capacity utilization was below 60 per cent in more than 900 industrial products (Lardy 1998: 81). And as for the losses of the SOEs, the rate at which bad debts were accumulating rose from 50 to 60 billion yuan in 1995, to over 200 billion yuan ($24 billion) in 1998 (Pomfret 1999). It was not surprising that despite reports of 7.8 per cent growth in 1997, President Jiang Zemin remarked in January 1999 that the country faced an economic slowdown (Rosenthal 1999), and Premier Zhu Rongji told the tenth National Peoples' Congress 2 months later that China faced a grim environment at home and abroad (*International Herald Tribune* 1999).

One of the few economists who came close to saying so was Thomas Rawski, then a professor at the University of Pittsburgh. In a series of articles written in 2001 and 2002, Rawski wondered how China had managed to increase its GDP between 1997 and 2000 by 24.7 per cent, when its energy consumption declined by 12.8 per cent. Rawski also pointed out several other anomalies. For instance, the official estimate of the growth of industrial production in 1998, of 10.75 per cent, is hard to reconcile with the fact that growth had exceeded 10 per cent in only 14 out of 94 main sectors of production, and had actually registered an absolute decline in 53 sectors. It is similarly hard to reconcile the increase in total fixed investment of 13.7 per cent a year with an increase in consumption of steel and cement of 5 per cent. Rawski concluded that China's actual rate of growth was not more than 2.2 per cent in 1998, 2.5 per cent in 1999, 3 per cent in 2000 and 4 per cent in 2001 (Rawski 2001 and Jha 2002: 135–148).

Rawski's observations created a storm that took him by surprise. Yakov Berger, chief of research at the Russian Academy of Sciences' Institute of Far Eastern Affairs, described him as a 'trouble maker' (Berger 2003). A number of Chinese economists pointed out that GDP growth had exceeded the rise in energy consumption, in South Korea, Japan and other countries by a wide margin on several occasions in the 1970s and 1980s. This argument was not convincing because, in the same period, there were several years in which energy consumption exceeded growth by a substantial margin. The two to-gether therefore gave a much more modest increase in the energy efficiency of growth. China's case was different not only because the discrepancy between energy consumption and GDP growth suddenly increased to mind-boggling levels between 1996 and 2001, but also because in the two worst years of the recession, 1997 and 1998, the official statistics would have us believe that the economy grew by 8.2 per cent a year when energy consumption declined in absolute terms by 2.4 per cent a year.[6]

Another not very convincing explanation was that this was the result of a surge of plant modernization during the investment boom of the early 1990s. But the one that most economists abroad as well as in China eventually accepted was that during the second half of the 1990s, coal production had gone underground after the central government asked the local administrations in 1997 to close down small coal mines because of their appalling safety record.[7] Coal accounted for 70 per cent of the total consumption of energy in the second half of the 1990s. Hiding some of its output would therefore be sufficient to explain the sharp reversal of energy growth.

But this argument too lost some of its plausibility when the National Bureau of Statistics published revised figures in the *China Statistical Yearbook* (CSY) 2006, for total energy consumption from 1999 till 2004 and simultaneously increased the estimate of coal consumption in 2005 by 30.7 per cent without explaining why it had done so. In CSY 2005, energy consumption had been shown to have declined by 6.4 per cent between 1997 and 2000. The CSY 2006 brought this figure down to a mere 0.2 per cent. This estimate was itself a good deal lower than the 12.8 per cent decline cited by Rawski using earlier official estimates and suggests that there had already been one exercise in unearthing the previously concealed consumption of coal. The change in the data in the CSY 2006, which brought down the decline over these 4 years further to a mere 0.2 per cent was the product of a second exercise. While revising the data for coal production may have been the main cause of the upward revision, it is difficult not to suspect that the incompatibility of an 8 per cent growth of GDP with a substantial decline in energy consumption, pointed out by Rawski and others, had not led to a retrospective cleaning up of the data. But even the second adjustment did not eliminate the anomaly, for it only reduced the decline in energy consumption over these 4 years from 6.4 to 0.2 per cent!

What Do the Data on Inputs Have to Say?

If China's energy consumption estimates are contested, what does the consumption of other inputs have to say? Table 4.2 presents a detailed picture of changes in the consumption of seven crucial inputs: labour, capital, total energy, electrical energy, steel, cement and soda ash. Table 4.3 compares changes in the rate of growth GDP (output) with other important indicators such as two indices of prices and the energy efficiency of growth.

The following tables leave one in little doubt that the 'slowdown' of 1996–2001 was far more severe than what the official data concede. Both tables show a sharp deceleration in the consumption of inputs and a sharp fall in demand in consumer demand (reflected in process) after 1995 which lasted till 2001. They also highlight the complete disconnect between the estimate of GDP growth and the growth in consumption of inputs. Between 1997 and 2000 the growth of consumption of not a single input came anywhere near the claimed growth of output. What is more, at the height of the recession, four of the indicators: industrial employment, energy and consumer and ex-factory prices, all went into negative territory. It is difficult to see how this can be called a 'slowdown', much less a 'soft landing'.

Table 4.2: Consumption of Primary Inputs and Key Intermediate Products Used in Manufacture 1978–2004, Annual Growth

Year	GDP	Employment (Industry)	Investment in FA	Consumption Energy Total	Consumption Energy Electrical	Consumption of Rolled Steel	Consumption of Cement	Consumption of Soda Ash
	1	2	3	4	5	6	7	8
1978–80	7.7	2.7		—	—			
1981–85	11.0	5.1	24	5.0	—			
1986–88	10.4	3.8*	23.2	6.6♣	9.0**			
1989	4.2	-1.1♣	-7.2	4.2	7.3			
1990	4.2	0.9♣	2.4	1.8	6.2			
1991	9.1	2.5	23.8	5.1	9.2	9.5	18.5	8.1
1992	14.1	3.0	60.6	5.2	11.5	19.0	22.0	7.8
1993	13.1	2.1	45.4	6.3	11.0	16.6	20.0	18.5
1994	12.6	3.4	30.4	5.8	9.9	9.0	14	7.5
1995	9.0	2.0	17.4	6.9	8.2	6.5	13	19.0
1996	9.8	-0.4	14.5	5.9	7.4	6.0	3.3	7.2
1997	8.6	-1.5	8.9	-0.8	4.8	6.6	4.4	3.2
1998	7.8	-2.0	13.9	-4.1	2.8	7.6	7.4	2.3
1999	7.2	-2.5	5.1	-1.6 (1.2)	6.1	12.5	4.4	3.6
2000	8.4	-0.8	10.3	0.1 (3.5)	9.5	8.5	4.1	3.2
2001	7.2	+0.4	13.1	3.5 (3.3)	8.6	22.0	10.5	1.8
2002	8.9	2.8	16.9	9.9 (6.0)	11.6	20.0	9.5	5.3
2003	10.1	1.8	27.6	(15.3)	16.5	2.5	18	16.7
2004	9.9	5.2	26.2	15.2 (16.1)	14.5	32.0	11.5	33
2005	10.2	6.9	26.7	—(9.9)	—(13.5)	19.2	10.2	8.6
2006♣	11.1	6.3	23.7	9.6	14.6	24.1	15.7	9.8

Sources: The figures in brackets above are taken from the *China Statistical Yearbook* 2006. All the remaining figures, except those specifically marked otherwise, are from *China Statistical Yearbook* 2005.

Notes: *Average for 1986–87; **1985 only.
♣Taken/calculated from CSY 2007.

Table 4.3: Indicators of Economic Performance, 1978–2004, Annual Growth

Year	GDP	Consumer Price	Ex-factory Price	dE/dY	dE(el)/dY
Column	1	2	3	4	5
1978–80	7.7	—	—	0.45	—
1981–85	11.0	9.3**	8.7**	0.63	
1986–88	10.4	18.8***	—	1.02	0.80**
1989	4.2	18.0	18.6	0.47	1.78
1990	4.2	3.1	4.1	0.55	1.63
1991	9.1	3.4	6.2	0.37	1.00
1992	14.1	6.4	6.8	0.21	0.81
1993	13.1	14.7	24.3	0.46	0.70
1994	12.6	24.1	19.5	0.66	0.79
1995	9.0	17.1	14.9	0.62	0.78
1996	9.8	8.3	2.9	NC	0.77
1997	8.6	2.8	–0.3	NC	0.55
1998	7.8	–0.8	–4.1	NC	0.36
1999	7.2	–1.4	–2.4	0.02	0.86
2000	8.4	+0.4	+2.8	0.47	1.19
2001	7.2	+0.7	–1.3	1.19	1.15
2002	8.9	–0.8	–2.2	1.61	1.40
2003	10.1	+0.9	2.3	1.60	1.74
2004	9.9	3.3	6.1	1.53	1.53
2005	10.2	1.8	4.9♣	1.02♣	1.30♣
2006♣♣	11.1	1.5	3.0	0.87	1.32

Source: *China Statistical Yearbook* 2005.

Notes: **1985 only; ***Figure for 1988; NC = not calculable; ♣Taken/
calculated from CSY 1996; ♣♣Data obtained from CSY 2007,
Table 7.8. There are minor differences between the data for 2003 in CSY
2006 and 2007.
dE = annual increase in total energy consumption.
dE(el) = annual increase in electricity consumption.
dY = annual increase in GDP.

   The above tables therefore confirm the conclusions of Zhang, Li
and Gan mentioned earlier. Enterprise, township, county, prefectural,
city and provincial governments feel no qualms about reporting the
achievement (or overachievement) of targets, but are reluctant to
report that they have failed to meet them. This translates into a pronounced upward bias in their estimates of output during economic
downturns.

5

'Cadre' Capitalism

The third, and the most misleading, myth is that China owes its near-miraculous performance to privatization. According to this version of events, while the state-owned enterprises (SOEs) failed to meet the challenge posed by the phased dismantling of the planned economy and the emergence of competitive product markets, a newly born 'non-state' or 'private' sector rediscovered the Chinese genius for enterprise and led the explosion of growth that followed. So successful was this new sector that unlike Russia, most of Eastern Europe and many other nations in transition, structural adjustment did not lead to even a temporary collapse of the economy or hardship to the people. On the contrary, the economic growth that followed was not only spectacular but also extraordinarily smooth. James A. Dorn, vice-president of the Washington-based Cato Institute, summed up China's achievements and unfinished tasks at a round table discussion in 2003 as follows:

> The great success of private and cooperative enterprises over the past 25 years—they now account for more than two-thirds of the value of industrial output—has resulted in official recognition of the importance of the non-state sector as an engine of economic growth. Article 11 of the Chinese Constitution, amended in 1999, now reads: 'Individual, private and other non-public economies that exist within the limits prescribed by law are major components of the socialist market economy.

Private firms were illegal in 1978 and SOEs dominated the economic landscape. Today there are nearly 2 million private enterprises employing more than 24 million workers, and the number of private enterprises is growing by more than 30 per cent per year. In Shanghai and other coastal cities, SOEs are becoming small islands in a sea of private enterprise. Much of the growth of the private sector has been spontaneous, in the sense that privatization took place without central direction as opportunities for trade increased, especially in the special economic zones (SEZs). Local jurisdictions were allowed to experiment with new ownership forms, and when they were successful, others sought to imitate that success. Only later did the central authorities put their stamp of approval on the institutional innovations.

The growth of private enterprise has occurred despite the lack of transparent legal title and restrictions on access to state bank credit. Informal private capital markets have evolved to fund the private sector and overseas Chinese have been an important source of investment funds. The strong performance of provinces with greater economic freedom, such as Fujian, Guangdong and Zhejiang, has created a new middle class and a demand for better government and more secure property rights.

Capitalists are now free to join the Chinese Communist Party (CCP), and several well-known private entrepreneurs are already members of the National Peoples' Congress. As more entrepreneurs join the party, there will be mounting pressure to change the status quo. At the 16th National Congress of the CCP in November 2002, President Jiang Zemin gave a clear signal that the private sector is an important part of China's future. He said, 'We need to respect and protect all work that is good for the people and society and improve the legal system for protecting private property'. The party charter now includes 'The Three Represents,' a doctrine that commits the party to embrace the fundamental interests of the majority of the people, not just the proletariat.

Chinese citizens can now own their own businesses, buy shares of stock, travel widely, hold long-term land use rights, own their homes and work for non-state firms. The depoliticization of economic life is far from complete, but the changes thus far have created new mindsets and expanded individual choice. The many restrictions and human rights violations that remain should not detract from the progress China has made since 1978, in raising the standard of living for millions of people and giving rebirth to civil society.[1]

To ascribe success to the acceptance of orthodox prescriptions for policy reform, 'policy entrepreneurs'[2] in the think tanks and international agencies have drawn four false analogies between China's transformation into a market economy and that of traditional pre-capitalist and mixed economies like India.

- The first is to characterize the proliferation of the new ventures from the mid-1980s in what has come to be called the 'non-state' sector, as the birth of a competitive market economy.
- The second is to equate the non-state sector with the private sector of a market economy.[3]
- The third is to deny that the economic slowdown after 1995 was a recession and to insist that it was a 'soft landing'.
- The fourth is to characterize the transfer of SOEs and collectives to non-state and in some cases, private entrepreneurs; this began in 1994 and became official policy in 1997, as part of a deliberate, planned strategy to improve the efficiency of the economy and to create the entrepreneurial class that China needs to sustain its transition to a market economy.

In reality, nothing could be further from the truth. The proliferation of enterprises was not driven by competition but its exact opposite, *the exercise of state power.* All that changed after liberalization was that, instead of the power to invest being centralized in Beijing, it began to be exercised in addition, by five tiers of local administration—province, prefecture, city, county and township, and their urban counterparts. Even the SOEs joined in the race to invest, and set up subsidiary enterprises, under the guise of urban collectives. Between 1978 and 1995, even as the policy-makers in Beijing were dismantling the command economy by winding up the planning system, lifting price and distribution controls on products, installing a taxation system that encouraged enterprise autonomy by leaving the surplus in the hands[4] of the enterprise managers, freeing the labour market and establishing a market for the shares of SOEs as a prelude to liberalizing the capital market, ministries and departments in both the central and the provincial governments were adding pell-mell to the number of SOEs. In 1978, there had been 83,700 state-owned industrial enterprises in the country employing 31.39 million workers. Eighteen years later, their number had grown to 113,800 and they employed 42.77 million workers (Maddison 1998: 81). This was reflected in the number of persons employed by the SOEs. This rose from 77.4 million in 1978 to 109.6 million in 1995 (*China Statistical Yearbook* 2005). There were thus 30,000 more state-owned industrial enterprises in 1996 after 18 years of reform employing one and a half times the number of workers as there had been at the beginning.

But the truly mind-boggling growth of the state took place under the aegis of the prefecture, county and township administrations. Between 1978 and 1996, the number of so-called 'non-state' industrial enterprises, nine-tenths of which were promoted by the townships, grew from 244,700 to 7.87 million (Maddison 1998: 81). The term 'non-state' only meant a freedom from the social obligations of the SOEs, but not from state ownership.

Dorn's equation of the 'non-state' sector with a sort of private sector glosses over a critical difference between the two: while the private investor runs a risk because he invests his own money, and is therefore subject to the discipline of the market, the cadres of the Chinese party that were responsible for this explosion of investment ran no risk. Investment was made fatally easy for them by the state's continuing monopoly of the banking system. Till 1998, this made the local bank manager a direct subordinate of the local party committee and its all-powerful secretary. Even after reforms in that year which were supposed to make bank managers independent of the local party committee and answerable only to the next level in their own hierarchy, the power of the party secretary and other members of the party committee made it difficult for them to deny his demands.[5]

As is explained in greater detail in the next chapters, China owes not only its rapid growth but also the rapid, and surprising, growth of social discontent to this single, hugely important feature of its transition to the market. For the motive that drove the investment was not to earn profit, but to extract a form of 'rent', i.e. kickbacks from the exercise by the party cadres of their power to sanction investment. Profit is the reward earned for taking entrepreneurial risk. It is taken out by the entrepreneur from a surplus created *for* society, by the success of his investment. It therefore commands respect even when that is grudgingly given. Rent, by contrast, is an extraction *from* the capital and not from its fruits. It is taken, in one form or another, before the investment takes place and therefore involves taking no risk. It therefore enjoys none of the legitimacy that genuine profit does. When the extraction is made possible through the misuse of state power, it endangers the legitimacy of the entire political system. What happened in China was therefore as different from genuine privatization as chalk from cheese. He Qinliang, one of the early, and most scathing, critics of the rent-seeking society that China was actually building described it as follows:

> Throughout the seventeen years of economic reform in China…the fact that the state still commands control over huge amounts of resources ha(s) produced inviting targets for classical 'rent-seeking behavior' (*xunzu huodong*). This has included a major form of illegal activity by less than scrupulous government officials who exploit their administrative authority and command over certain economic sectors to seek out and receive massive personal 'commission fees' *as payment for their role in allowing the illicit stripping of state-owned assets and property. In an assessment of the overall social and political impact of the seventeen years of reform, the most unacceptable development in the eyes of the average citizen has been the enormous growth in corruption and personal enrichment by these officials at the public's expense.* [emphasis added] (He Qinliang 2000b: 49)

Coming to the second false analogy, the whirlwind growth of China's 'non-state' sector has been praised by scholars in the West and international agencies, as a welcome shift from a centrally planned and state-owned to a market-driven and privately owned economy. Indeed, in an even more loose but increasingly frequent use of the term, the 'non-state' sector has been equated with the private sector and the creation of enterprises that do not enjoy the legislated safety net of the communist era, as 'privatization'.[6] This description is not only profoundly misleading for the reason given above but also because it deliberately slurs over the moral and political issues that this type of growth has raised, within China itself. Till the end of the 1990s, China had very little enterprise that could truly be called private, in the Western sense of the term. The huge spurt in investment that took place after 1984 had occurred almost entirely under state auspices. Township and county administrations did it by setting up rural and urban collectives, and smaller SOEs. Provincial and city governments set up new SOEs as well as a variety of trust and holding companies that in turn set up enterprises owned by them. The common feature of both was the absence of true privatization, because that would have meant the loss of control over the enterprises and their funds by the concerned cadres. In all these cases, therefore, the ultimate owner was the state.

Although private entrepreneurship has been officially encouraged since the late 1990s, when President Jiang Zemin opened membership of the Communist Party to private entrepreneurs in his policy of 'Three Represents', China still has as many as 20 forms of ownership, of which private firms and the SOEs are the two ends of the spectrum. In numerical terms, the vast majority of the enterprises fall in between, in a set of messy compromises between private and public, which are a paradise for speculators and asset strippers, because they make it fatally easy for the managers to cream away profits of the successful enterprises and pass on losses to the state.

In sharp contrast to Russia and Eastern Europe, in China the overwhelming majority of sales to private individuals have been to workers and managers—so-called 'insider privatization' (Li and Rozelle 2003). Managers have often bought out the shares of the workers. So ultimately the managers, along with relatives and friends, have emerged as the true owners of companies that remain, in name at least, workers collectives.[7] Feng Chen, who undertook a detailed study of three firms in central China, concluded:

> [P]rivatization in China has been carried out in opaque ways, with little regard to the principles of fairness and justice. The government has never made it an official national policy and no national legislation exists to dictate the process. There are only a few government guidelines, which are far from clear and whose enforcement is highly problematic. Local authorities and SOE managers are granted considerable discretionary power to decide how factory property is handled; workers, on the other hand, are totally excluded from the process. Under such arrangements, privatization has taken two forms. The first, a *de facto* form of privatization, is similar to what is called 'spontaneous privatization' and occurred in the post-communist countries at the beginning of the regime transformation. In this process, SOE managers typically establish their own companies into which they siphon state assets through various dubious means, or manage to control the share of the existing SOEs in other ways. *De jure* privatization, which is directly relevant to this case study, is a formal transfer of state assets to private hands. The transaction is often arbitrary and poorly regulated, involving complicity among SOE managers, private buyers and local officials in carving up benefits at the expense of workers. Formal procedures for the transfer of state property (such as the approval of Staff and Workers' Councils) are either deliberately ignored or manipulated against labour interests. Compensation to workers is often reduced to the lowest level possible. (Chen 2006)

The need to identify the recession that hit the Chinese economy after 1995 as a 'soft landing'—the third false analogy—arises from the second analogy discussed above. If the huge spurt in investment between 1985 and 1995 was the result of privatization, which is necessarily good for the economy, then it becomes much harder to admit that it did untold harm to the Chinese economy by piling up excess capacity, causing huge waste and pushing it into a severe recession at the precise moment when the central government was gearing itself up to restructure the SOEs left over from the communist period. By far, the simpler course is to deny that there was a recession. That is what the Chinese government did and continues to do. Most foreign scholars have fallen in line with its characterization. The evidence in favour of there having been a recession is discussed in greater detail in Chapter 6.[8]

Subscribing to the third misleading analogy makes it necessary to subscribe to the fourth—that the rapid privatization of all but a small number of large SOEs in the second half of the 90s was a product of choice and not compulsion. In reality, the hectic privatization that began in 1997 was a product of the recession that set in at the end of the previous year. Privatization began in a small way in 1993 but gathered momentum rapidly after the government of Jiang Zemin and Zhu Rongji sanctioned a 3-year structural adjustment programme, in 1998. From 1997, when the two leaders first announced their decision to restructure the SOE, both the central and the local authorities began to reduce the number of SOEs in a variety of ways. At the higher levels of administrative control, the centre, the province, the prefecture and the county, its vast majority were either sold to their workers and managers or 'folded into' other more profitable state-owned or 'non-state', but still officially state-owned enterprises. At the township level, a majority were also sold, in whole or part, to individuals connected with the enterprise.

All these sales were indiscriminately hailed as proof of China's firm resolve to consolidate its industrial structure under private ownership and emerge as a lean and highly competitive industrial economy, and that may well have been Beijing's original intention. But the onset of recession in 1997 turned privatization into an altogether different exercise. Local authorities whose powers of taxation and fee fixation had been drastically curtailed by a sweeping reform of the taxation system in 1994 had found themselves pressed for resources, even before the recession began. When demand began to disappear and prices began to fall in late 1996 and early 1997, the enterprises they had set up became white elephants. They therefore saw in 'privatization' a heaven-sent opportunity, to pass the responsibility for reviving or dissolving them to others—usually their managers and workers.[9] Before the recession began, workers had bought shares in their enterprises willingly. In a first experiment in the complete privatization of 210 small and medium enterprises in Zhucheng, a town in Shandong, in 1994, the workers willingly paid 1,000 yuan per share to buy between two and five shares in their enterprises. Later, presumably when profits began to flag, many of them had second thoughts. But since the shares could not be sold to outsiders, most of them sold their shares to the managers or others within the enterprise and managed to make a small profit (OECD 2000: 45). But as the recession deepened and more and more of the small and medium-sized enterprises began to fail,[10] the sale of shares to the workers began to acquire a coercive tinge. In a similar sale, four years later, when the recession was at its height, workers in a 700-employee plant were forced to buy 5,000 yuan worth of shares each, with the threat that if they did not do so, they would lose their jobs and be denied of all the benefits that they were entitled to. A hundred or so of them refused and resorted to one of the early collective actions of the post-reform period (Kai 2002: 334).

These misleading analogies have allowed the international financial institutions, and liberal economists in the West, to applaud the development of a state–economy relationship that has been causing mounting anxiety among China's intellectuals and senior party officials for more than a decade; for the gradual shift from a socialist to a market economy has created not a true market economy, but a hybrid that combines the worst features of state control with some of the most exploitative features of a market economy. This is what Minxin Pei has called the 'Decentralized Predatory State'.[11] Cadres in the Chinese state administration and Communist Party have combined their political control over key economic resources with the growing economic freedom to buy, sell and invest, to create a predator state and extract rent, either as wealth or as advancement, within the state and party hierarchies. In the words of two Chinese scholars, Chen Guidi and Wu Chuntao, '*Once our cadres were turned into a special interest class, it was inevitable that their interests would be in competition with those of the masses*' (Guidi and Chuntao 2005).

The Growing Inefficiency of Growth

The recession hit rock-bottom in 1998–2000 but recovery began, unambiguously, only in 2002, when industrial employment recorded its first sharp increase of 2.8 per cent, and energy consumption began to rise sharply once again. Consumer prices, ex-factory prices and the investment deflator moved unambiguously into positive territory a year later. From that year onwards China's recovery strengthened at the same explosive pace that it had witnessed in the early 1990s and in 2005, the economy began, once again, to overheat. But this second recovery was different from that of the early 1990s, for Chinese growth had ceased to be material and energy efficient.

This is apparent from Table 4.2. In column number 4, if one ignores the corrupted data for 1996–2000, the increase in energy consumption which was needed to obtain a unit increase in the growth of gross domestic product (GDP) remains fairly stable between 0.45 and 0.66 till 1995. Column number 5 gives a similar picture for the consumption of electrical energy. The only exceptions were in the years 1989 and 1990, when the incremental electrical energy to GDP ratio shot up because of a disproportionate decline in its use in manufacture. But when growth resumed in 2002, the increase in energy consumption began, regularly, to exceed the increase in GDP. The government's concern was reflected in its commitment to reduce energy consumption per unit of GDP by 4 per cent a year, in the Five Year Plan between 2005 and 2010. But it received a rude shock when it found that energy consumption had grown by 0.8 per cent *more* than the GDP in the first half of 2006.[12]

There was a similar increase in the use of other key industrial inputs as Table 5.1 shows.

Table 5.1: Materials Intensity of Growth in China (in percentage)

Year	GDP	Rolled Steel	Cement	Plate Glass	Soda Ash	Plastics
1980–85	66	36	83	100	25	38
2000–04	41	83	44	51	56	52

Source: Calculated from *China Statistical Yearbook* 2005, Tables 14–19.

Thus, the consumption coefficient for steel per percentage increase of the GDP rose from 0.54 in 1980–85 to 2.02 in 2000–04 and that of soda ash, a base material in the chemicals industry, rose from

0.37 to 1.36. The consumption coefficient of plastics rose equally sharply from 0.58 to 1.27. The consumption of cement and plate glass, both prime building materials especially for office buildings, showed a more mixed trend, because of its close correlation with booms and recessions in the building industry. During the early years of the recovery, this was still suffering from the overhang of unsold apartments and office space left over by the previous boom. The ratio of cement consumption to GDP growth had risen sharply from 1.26 in 1980–85 to 1.74 in 1990–95, before falling back to 1.07 in 2000–04. The consumption of plate glass, a prime office building material, showed a similar trend. The high figure for 1990–95 reflects the frenzy of overbuilding that followed the opening of thousand of SEZs and development zones in the late 1980s and early 1990s. In 1997, Chinese investors found themselves saddled with a huge property bubble of unsold flats and office space.

China's experience is in striking contrast to that of India, where, as Table 5.2 shows, there has been a decrease in the incremental use of energy and raw materials for growth after the economy was liberalized in 1991.

Table 5.2: Materials Intensity of Growth in India (in percentage)

Year**	GDP	Energy	Finished Steel	Cement
1980–85	32	29	44	78 (50)*
2000–05	33	21	41	52

Source: Ministry of Finance, Government of India Economic Surveys 1995–96 and 2006–07.

Notes: *The high figure here probably reflects the emergence of clandestine production and sales after cement price and distribution controls were lifted in 1981. **The fiscal year begins on 1 April, so these data relate to 1 April of the given year till 31 March of the next year.

The conclusion is inescapable: Since the end of the 1980s China's growth has become progressively more raw materials-intensive. Only its inflated growth figures, especially after 1995, have hidden this from view. Can China sustain its present rate of growth, or even a somewhat lower average rate, if it needs ever larger amounts of capital, energy and raw materials to sustain dollar of increase in its GDP? These trends are visible even if one accepts the official rate of growth of GDP. But they become starkly apparent if one concludes from the data on the consumption of inputs, prices, investment and raw materials consumption, that there was a sharp recession after 1996 that lasted till at least 2000, and brought down the growth rate between 1995 and 2000 substantially below the official estimate. But if we lower the growth rate between 1995 and 2000 to the 4.2 per cent recorded in 1989 and 1990, then in the period 1995 till 2004 a 73 per cent growth of GDP required a 167 per cent increase in the consumption of steel, an 81 per cent increase in the consumption of cement, a 77 per cent increase in the consumption of plate glass, a 116 per cent increase in the consumption of soda ash and a 219 per cent increase in the consumption of plastics.[13]

The rising materials intensity of China's growth has become a matter of concern not only in international organizations and research institutes across the world but even more in China. In August 2005, shortly after China formalized its 11th Five Year Plan, Pan Yue, deputy environment minister, put the issue in stark terms in an interview in *Der Spiegel*: 'We are using too many raw materials to sustain this growth', he said. 'To produce goods worth US$ 10,000, for example, we need seven times more resources than Japan, nearly six times more than the US and, perhaps most embarrassingly, nearly three times more than India' (Ching 2005). He might have also added that China was using more than twice as much energy per dollar of GDP, measured in real consumption, than India.[14]

The 11th Plan set a target of bringing down the energy consumed per unit of incremental GDP by 20 per cent, that is by 4 per cent a year. The State National Development and Reform Commission (SDRC) turned this into a set of concrete goals in a report published in August 2006. Central to it was a reduction of the consumption of coal by 300 million metric tonnes a year. This accounted for 13.5 per cent of the energy consumed in 2005. But to do so, it warned, China would have to close down, install anti-pollution equipment, or otherwise modernize the vast majority of its 500,000 small and medium-sized coal-fired boilers. These consumed 400 million tonnes of coal each year and were responsible for most of the country's serious atmospheric pollution. Up to 70 million tonnes could be saved by upgrading the technology and management of these boilers.

Just how difficult it would be to achieve the Plan target was revealed when in the first half of 2006, the increase in energy consumption actually exceeded the growth of GDP by 0.8 per cent (Huang 2006b). Experts at the SDRC said it would take time for the energy saving measure the government was implementing to take effect, but other

Chinese energy experts are not so sanguine, and do not believe that the target can be met. On the contrary, Yu Cong, a researcher at the National Development and Reform Commission's Energy Research Institute predicted that energy consumption in the mainland economy would rise to about 5.6 billion tonnes of standard coal equivalent in 2020, which is almost double of a previous government projection. Ms Yu put the blame on energy hungry sectors, including iron and steel, building materials and chemical and petrochemical industries, which had shown signs of rapid expansion in the first half of this year (Tao 2006).

China's hunger for energy pales before its consumption of other key non-renewable resources. Table 5.3, which compares its consumption with that of the United States and India, tells its own story.

Table 5.3: Share of China, India and the US in World Consumption of Key Raw Materials (in percentage)

	China	India	United States
Metals 2005			
Aluminum	22.5	3.0	19.4
Copper	21.6	2.3	13.8
Lead	25.7	1.3	19.4
Nickel	15.2	0.9	9.5
Tin	33.3	2.2	12.1
Zinc	28.6	3.1	9.0
Iron ore	29.0	4.8	4.7
Steel production	31.5	3.5	8.5
Energy 2003	China	India	United States
Coal	32.9	7.1	20.6
Oil	7.4	3.4	25.3
Energy (total)	12.6	3.6	23.4
Electricity generation	11.4	3.8	24.3

Source: Winters and Yusuf 2006.

With one-tenth of the world's GDP in purchasing power terms, China is consuming between one-third and one-sixth of the world's traded raw materials including one-third of its coal, and one-eights of its total energy. It consumes substantially more than the US of everything except crude oil, despite the fact that it has barely 15 per cent of its GDP. And while this comparison is at least partly one of unlikes because the US is now largely a post-industrial society, the same cannot be said of India.[15] With 2.3 times India's purchasing power party (PPP)-GDP China consumes 7–20 times as much of every important primary raw material that enters world trade. These trends cannot be sustained indefinitely. The current pattern of development has therefore got to change. China, in effect, needs to repeat what it did after 1978—move back from capital intensive, investment-led, growth to a more balanced, more diversified and consumption-led pattern of growth (*Financial Times Editorial* 2006).

The Energy Crunch

Nowhere is the impending crisis more acute than in energy. China's and India's growing energy needs led the International Energy Agency to issue a warning in a report presented in London in November 2006, that world consumption of energy would rise by 53 per cent from 84 million barrels a day in 2005 to 116 million barrels per day by 2030. The developing countries, led by China and India, would account for 70 per cent of the increase (*India Abroad News Service* 2006).

China's energy needs are rising sharply at precisely the moment when the world has begun to sense that it will soon run out of oil. China was a net exporter of oil till 1993. Since then its imports have increased by leaps and bounds. In 2001, it imported 66 million tonnes. In 2004, the figure had risen to 101 million tonnes, in 2005 to 143 million tonnes (Qingyi 2006) and in 2006 to 158 million tonnes.[16] The International Energy Agency has estimated that based upon present trends, China could be importing 10 million barrels a day or more than half a billion tonnes a year by 2030, five times what it imported in 2004 (Holland 2005). By then the world will be close to running out of oil. Estimates made in 1983 suggest that by 2040, 80 per cent of the known oil reserves will have been consumed (Riva 1983). The unexpected emergence of China and India as major consumers has undoubtedly made that estimate too conservative today.

The Environment

High energy and raw materials use has combined to wreak havoc on the environment. In September 2006, the National Bureau of

Statistics and the State Environmental Protection Administration announced the first results of a long-term project to quantify the impact of growing pollution on the economy. It estimated the cost, in terms of sickness, health and lowered productivity, in 2004 alone, to be of the order of 3 per cent of economic output. To repair the damage that had already been done would cost China about 1.080 trillion yuan ($136 billion). That was equal to about 7 per cent of its GDP. As China's GDP per capita reaches the range of $1,000 to $3,000, the report concluded,

> ...society [which] has experienced frequent conflicts and can no longer bear the social problems caused by environmental pollution...Although (China's) brand of high consumption, high pollution and...high-risk development has had a certain historical use, our economy has now hit a bottleneck for resource and energy use. (McGregor 2006)

6

Why Purely Economic Remedies Have Not Worked

'Why is China so prodigal in its use of scarce raw materials? If the need to adopt a less material-intensive pattern of development, is so well understood, then why has the government in Beijing not taken steps to redress the balance already?' More pertinent still, *why did China drift back into capital and materials intensive growth in the early 1990s, after having got away from it in the 1980s?*

The generally accepted explanation is China's inability to break with its socialist–dirigiste past and the consequent incompleteness of its reforms, given by Carsten Holz and Tian Zhu of the Hong Kong University of Science and Technology. China's decision to 'ford the river by feeling the stones' left it with two interconnected but essentially distinct problems. The first was a huge legacy of increasingly non-viable enterprises that were neither closed down nor allowed to wither away because of the enormous social disruption that would have been caused. The second was that this industrial over-hang was itself exceedingly fragmented, with a huge number of sub-optimal scale plants and factories, most of which embodied obsolete technologies. Overcapitalized, overstaffed, burdened with an overhang of social obligations and prey to meddling by senior party cadres and a many-layered bureaucracy, these enterprises could neither adapt to the market nor compete with the rapidly growing new quasi-state or non-state sectors, such as the joint ventures, urban collectives, rural township and village enterprises and after 1996, a rapidly growing private sector. The economic slowdown, they pointed out led to a fall in the overall profitability of the state-owned enterprises (SOEs). In 1997, the profits of the profit makers exceeded the losses of the loss makers by a mere 42 billion yuan. This was 8 billion less than the net profit recorded in 1978. Even more dramatic was the fall in the return—defined in China as the operating surplus[1]—on the investment in total fixed assets. This plummeted from a not unhealthy 28 per cent in 1985 to 3.3 per cent in 1995.[2] By Western accounting standards, in 1995, after a decade of growth such as the world has never known, the entire state-owned sector was running at a loss! Yet, rather than let loss-making enterprises declare themselves bankrupt, the government repeatedly directed the banks to extend loans to them to help them tide over.[3]

The mounting losses of the SOEs thus triggered a crisis in the banking system, which found itself saddled with a rising portfolio of bad loans. By the mid-1990s, estimates of the bad loans by the state banks ranged from 20 per cent to about 50 per cent. The 20 per cent estimate of bad debts tended to cover only non-performing loans and loan losses, while the higher estimate usually included overdue loans. In 1995, an economist at the Central Party School suggested that 'according to the most conservative estimate, the share of non performing loans and unpaid interest in all bank loans was about 25 per cent; some scholars even think this figure to be around 47 per cent' (Holz and Zhu 2002: 71–109). Foreign credit-rating agencies were giving higher figures. For example, Moody's estimate for end-1996 was 35 to 70 per cent (ibid).

Since the surpluses of the SOEs were the state's prime source of revenue, their failure to grow in pace with the economy created a fiscal crisis. State revenues fell from 35 per cent of gross domestic product (GDP) in 1978 to 11 per cent in 1993. The state therefore plunged into deficit. In 1990, expenditures were running 10 per cent ahead of revenue. This rose to 23 per cent on an average, between 1995 and 2000. In 2000, the fiscal deficit amounted to 4.55 per cent of the GDP. A growing part was being used to finance current consumption (Holz and Zhu 2002: 74, Table 3).

The fiscal crisis led directly to a crisis in the social security system. The SOEs had the responsibility for looking after their workers but could not. Ideally, the government should have taken over the responsibility, but it was too strapped for cash to do so, while the banks were too preoccupied with meeting the *current* losses of the SOEs to make advances that could safeguard their future.

These three interlocking crises paralyzed the Chinese economic system. Nowhere was this reflected more clearly than in the frozen pattern of bank lending. In 1978, at the end of the socialist epoch, the SOEs accounted for 91.06 per cent of all bank loans. Agriculture received a paltry 6.25 per cent and collectives 2.69 per cent. Twenty-two years later, in 2000, the SOEs' share of output had dropped to a third of the GDP, but its share of loans had dropped to only 79 per cent. The share of agriculture had actually halved to 3.5 per cent. The entire non-state sector accounted for only 17 per cent of loans (Holz and Zhu 2002: 72, Table 1). Yet by 2000, the township and village enterprises alone accounted for 30 per cent of the GDP, more than half of industrial output and 40 per cent of exports (OECD 2003). Its need for investable funds was being met by a parallel, 'curbside' money market consisting of private bankers, SOEs that took cheap loans and re-lent them to the non-state sector and foreign invest-ors. But even the most generous estimate of its size would still place the availability of funds to this sector, at well under half of the total (Holz and Zhu 2002: 72).

The conclusions by Holz and Tian Zhu have been echoed in a more recent book, *Under New Ownership: Privatising China's State Owned Enterprises*, by Shahid Yusuf, Koru Nageshima and Dwight Perkins. The authors place the blame for China's wasteful development squarely on its decision to opt for incremental reform. China's rapid growth, they conclude, has been the result of massive investment, fi-nanced by large intersect oral transfers of resources (mainly from the rural to the urban sector), and not from increases in productivity. As a result economic growth has been extraordinarily expensive. The solution, according to the authors is for China to forego the luxury of gradual reform and privatize the remainder of the SOEs, as rapidly as possible (Yusuf et al. 2005).

Failure of Economic Remedies— State-owned Industry

The sense of urgency that informs the latter book, in particular, arises from a growing awareness that economic reforms of the kind, advo-cated by the International Monetary Fund and the World Bank for other transitional economies were proving infructuous in China. By the middle of 1998, China's leaders were fully aware of the in-tractable nature of the 'triple crisis'. The central government therefore embarked upon a spate of reforms to curtail the losses and subject the state and non-state sectors to the discipline of the market. The core of this reform was a massive reorganization of the state-owned industrial sector. In 1997, this consisted of 514 key enterprises at the apex of the pyramid, all of which were centrally owned, and another 4,286 large enterprises, 10,123 medium-sized enterprises and 59,465 small enterprises. The 4,800 key and large enterprises accounted for 70.08 per cent of industrial production and the medium-sized enterprises for 15.35 per cent of the output. The nearly 60,000 small enterprises accounted for only 14.57 per cent of output (Yusuf et al. 2005: 89). On 19 September 1997, the first plenum of the 15th Chinese Communist Party Central Committee adopted a 3-year programme of reform. The strategy it endorsed was one of 'seizing the big ones and letting go of the small ones'. Its objective was to convert the large and medium-sized enterprises into modern companies and help the loss-making among them to 'escape their difficulties'. This was a euphemism for adopting a variety of strategies, such as mergers, selective close down of lines of production and selling profitable lines of production, within an enterprise to generate the cash for closing down unprofitable lines, that were designed to avoid having to close them down altogether. In all, by the end of 2000, the central and the provincial governments had closed down only 301 large and medium-sized enterprises.

In the 3 years after the first plenum's directive, the central and provincial authorities reduced the number of industrial enterprises from 74,388 to 53,489. By the end of 2000, they had also selected 2,919 large enterprises for conversion into formal companies whose shares could be traded on the stock exchange, and converted 2005 of them. These included 440 of the 514 key enterprises and a large number of important provincially run enterprises. By the end of 2000, the number of loss-making enterprises, large and medium-sized enterprises, had been reduced from 6,599 to 1,800 (Yusuf et al. 2005: 89).

According to an official Chinese report, about 70 per cent of the improvement had resulted from the beginning of recovery in the economy after the recession of 1997–98, and the reflationary investment in infrastructure begun by Zhu Rongji in 1998 to combat it (Jha 2002: 152–54). This pushed up the overall profitability of the state sector from 1.96 per cent in 1998 to 7.36 per cent in 2000 (Holz and Zhu 2002: Table 5). But the damage done by the investment spree of the early 1990s had gone too deep to be cured in so short a period of time. By the end of 2000, another 1,836 large and medium-sized SOEs had slipped into the red (Holz and Zhu 2002: 89).

The small enterprises were left to the provincial authorities to deal with. These had already begun to reduce their number before the Three Year Plan was mooted by Premier Zhu Rongji in 1997. The endorsement from the top hastened the process. In all, more than 19,500 small enterprises were transferred to the non-state sector (Holz and Zhu 2002: 92).[4] The majority were sold to their employees; merged with, or folded into, other stronger enterprises; sold or merged piecemeal and encouraged to form joint ventures with foreign investors.

Failure of Economic Remedies—
the Banking System

The central government also made a determined attempt to resolve the problem created by the pile-up of non-performing loans (NPL). In 1998, it enacted sweeping reforms of the banking system with three objectives: to bring lending criteria more in line with international practice (including some increase in the cost of borrowing); to free the local branches of the commercial banks from the compulsion to obey local party cadres and extend loans as directed by them; and to enable the banks to clear their portfolios of dead assets and start with a clean slate. The first was a long-term goal and the Politburo and State Council recognized that it would do little to resolve the immediate crisis. To achieve the second objective, the government relied, almost exclusively, upon administrative fiat—a series of directives to the banks and provincial authorities. This was because a succession of reports from banks and government departments were virtually unanimous that the problem had arisen after reforms began, specifically in the frenzy to invest that occurred between 1991 and 1996, and was not a leftover of the communist era. In mid-1997, before the full magnitude of the Asian crisis became apparent, a research team at the headquarters of the Industrial and Commercial Bank of China had been preparing a research report on NPLs and local redundant investment. The report, first circulated internally among government officials, confirmed the existence of rampant redundant investment and put the blame for it on local (that is provincial, city and municipal) governments and the defective industrial policies of Zhu Rongji's predecessor, Li Peng (Shih 2004: 934–36). The key weakness of these policies was the subordination of the local banks to city and provincial and, to a lesser extent, township authorities. The autonomy that the various levels of the government enjoyed in making investment decisions made it possible for them to raise as much capital as they wanted, without incurring the financial risk that private entrepreneurs run in capitalist societies, of having the investment go sour. From the beginning therefore Zhu Rongji, who was to become the premier in the spring of 1998, was inclined towards a massive centralization of lending, and on placing absolute ceilings on loans and on permissible NPLs, to instill discipline into the financial system.

In October 1997, the Central Committee and the State Council jointly issued the 'Notice concerning deepening financial reform, rectifying financial order and preventing financial risk'. At one stroke of the pen, it removed local branches of the state banks and the Peoples' Bank of China (PBC) from the local party committees' jurisdiction and placed them under a newly formed Central Finance Work Committee. Hundreds of locally controlled trust and investment companies and underground banks were closed (Shih 2004: 934–36). This directive was implemented in 1998.

Provincial officials were outraged by this sudden surge of central power. Zhu had to offer words of comfort to the disgruntled local leaders: 'the centralization of monetary authority does not mean that we do not trust local officials. It is just that the centre and localities should each divide up our labour accordingly' (Shih 2004: 934–36). Besides these words, however, Zhu also offered two concessions to the provinces to stem their anger. First, he allowed the provinces to charter more local banks to help local development. This was merely a token gesture because Zhu Rongji had just closed down hundreds of local financial institutions and deprived local government control of the state banks. The second was a promise to use the re-centralized borrowing power to continue the development of the central and Western zones of the country (Shih 2004: 933–34).

To resolve the bad loans problem, the government created four Asset Management Companies in 1999 that took over 1.4 trillion of bad loans. These amounted to 21 per cent of their total portfolios. With a clean slate, the banks were expected to record profits on the remainder of their portfolios and use these to write off 2–4 per cent of the bad debts every year. They were also expected to sell as much of the bad debt as possible to recover some part of the loss. But the consequences of the decisions that had already been taken continued to haunt the policy-makers. As China went into recession, with steep declines in prices and mounting stocks of unsold goods, more and more loans went bad. Between 1998 and 2002, banks accumulated another 1.7 trillion RMB of bad loans on their books (Pei 2006: 117). In March 2001, the Bank of China broke ranks with the other commercial banks and admitted that 28.78 per cent of its loans were 'non-performing'. In November, the governor of the PBC estimated that NPLs exceeded 26 per cent of all loans. Thus, by early 2003, the total had risen to an estimated 3.3 trillion yuan. That was 37 per cent of the GDP in 2000 (Shih 2004).

The only difference that the 1998 reforms made was to transfer the power to dictate bank lending from the provincial authorities, who had progressively usurped it during the decade of 1985–95, back to the central bureaucracy. This brought the banks only a temporary and to some extent illusory reprieve from insolvency. Central control meant that a disproportionate share of the fresh loans was invested in long-term projects designed to create fixed assets. These did not create bad loans in the immediate future and so allowed bank managers to show a decline in their NPL ratio, but in China's climate of all-pervasive overinvestment, these too were extremely risky in the long run. For instance, no less than 1.5 trillion RMB was allocated for projects in western China. A high percentage continued to be ploughed into real estate construction, despite the fact that only 5 per cent of these projects were capable of paying back both the interest and the principal, while 20 per cent could pay back neither.[5] Bank managers who were interviewed by scholars also said that the pressure to achieve a 7–8 per cent growth target in the late 1990s had compelled them to accept third and fourth tier projects (Shih 2004).

Banking officials fell in readily with these long-term investment programmes, not because they were any less politically driven or less risky but because being long-term, the loans they gave would not become due for many years. As a result, the ratio of advances to NPLs could rise steadily for several years, without any increase in NPLs. Centralization of lending and the concentration on long-term loans had postponed the banking crisis, not solved its underlying causes. As one Chinese scholar, Victor Shih, put it:

> Reform is crossing the river by feeling for stones (*moshi guohe*). Yet, the stones that Chinese leaders feel for are not sound economic policies but political survival. The current that threatens to topple leaders is not policy failure but political attack. To stand firm on the stones, leaders do not hesitate to move sideways or even step back away from the current. The objective is to remain standing, not necessarily to cross the river. (Shih 2004: 922)

Shih's misgivings proved well founded. In 2002, even as China entered its next hectic investment boom, the secondary and tertiary effects of the recession years continued to work their way through the banking system. The volume of non-performing loans began to pile-up again. When these reached 26.2 per cent of advances in 2002, the government felt obliged to step in once again. Late in 2003, using $60 billion of foreign exchange reserves, the Ministry of Finance created Huijin, a holding company, which bought shares in three of the four big state-owned commercial banks to recapitalize them. The government also transferred 780 billion yuan of their fresh NPLs to the Asset Management Corporations. These measures enabled the state-owned commercial banks to lower their NPL ratio from 26 per cent in 2002 to 10.5 per cent in 2005 (Ma 2007). But this improvement too may turn out to be short lived.

By 2002, the crisis of insolvency caused by the recession had spread from the state-owned to the new, more or less private, banking system that had been growing up side by side with the state commercial banks. More and more of them were facing bankruptcy. Beijing was therefore left with no option but to bale these out too. The bale out began when the PBC—the Central Bank—bought a large chunk of the non-performing assets of the Bank of Communications, the country's fifth largest bank, at half price and recapitalized it to the tune of 35 billion yuan. This was the beginning of a new strategy in which the government sought to infuse discipline, and freedom from the dictates of party officials, into the banking system, by privatizing it. The initial purchase by the PBC was intended to lead the way for the sale of shares in the second tier city banks to private and foreign investors. Thus the PBC's purchase was followed by the purchases by other stakeholders including Huijin, the National Social Security Fund, and the Hong Kong and Shanghai Bank which made a

15 billion yuan purchase, probably the first of its kind. This opened the way for foreign investment in the banking sector and by 2006, foreign banks had invested $17 billion in 19 Chinese banks.

That was not the end of the story. By 2004, virtually all 34,000 Regional Credit Co-operatives (RCCs) of the country, and all but a handful of its second tier city commercial banks, were insolvent or heading towards it. The RCCs had been driven there partly by the failure of township and village enterprises (TVEs) to pay back their loans, and partly by the tax reforms of 1998, in which the central government had wound up the rural credit foundations—informal banking institutions that had been set up by the TVE administrations throughout the country—to raise money for enterprises that they had hoped would generate surplus that would help to finance the township budgets (Ong 2006). Had growth continued at the high levels as that of the early 1990s, their gamble might well have paid off, but in the prolonged economic slowdown and price deflation that began in 1997 (the prices fell for 53 months in a row), it failed. Most of these enterprises made losses and the RCFs speedily became insolvent. The government was therefore forced to take over 336 billion yuan of their debt and, in addition, give them another 104 billion yuan to bring them up to the capital adequacy norms it had set. It also baled out the city commercial banks to the tune of 36 billion yuan (Ong 2006).

An indication of how seriously the assets created by the investment boom of the early 1990s had been eroded in the succeeding recession can be gathered from the utter failure of the Asset Management Companies, set up in 1998, to get any significant amount back from the sale of the older stock of NPLs. By February 2007, they had been able to dispose off 1.12 trillion of the 1.4 trillion yuan of bad debt that they had bought from the four original commercial banks but had been able to recover only 211 billion yuan from their sale. This was most probably not sufficient to cover the interest on the debt (Ong 2006).

2002–07: Out of Control

By 2001, therefore the central government had tried just about every economic remedy it could think of to make the economy viable and self-regulating. It had merged, closed or transformed thousands of companies into limited liability companies to make them more market oriented; laid off or transferred 40 million state employees to the non-state sector, recaptured control of the banking system from local authorities, purged the banks of the bad debts, progressively introduced modern instruments of monetary control, allowed the rise of private banks and drawn in foreign direct investment into the existing state and provincial banks to make their managers more commercially minded and accountable. These reforms had led to an improvement in the overall performance of the state sector and reduction of losses in the banking system. But the reforms did not touch the core of the problem, which was the continuing divorce of power from responsibility in the state-owned sector, that is, the power to take loans without the responsibility to pay them back. As a result, no sooner did the recession end, in 2001, than the Chinese economy began to repeat the mistakes of the early 1990s all over again.

The recession (or slowdown) ended in 2001 and within a year, China was powering forward again. But as had happened in 1992, within two short years of the turn around, history began to repeat itself and the Chinese economy began to overheat again. Bank lending grew at an accelerating rate towards the end of 2002 and during the first half of 2003, bank credit expanded by 23 per cent, much too rapidly to be sustainable. Moreover, loans by state-owned banks increased more rapidly than those by other types of banks, accounting for 62 per cent of the increase. Fixed investment had been growing strongly for several years under Zhu Rongji's programme, to counter the recession by promoting infrastructure construction and had already reached the extremely high level of 42 per cent of GDP in 2002. Even so, fixed investment jumped further during the first half of 2003, increasing at a rate of 31 per cent. The cause, as in 1992–94, was once again that the provincial administrations ran away with investment. During the first half of 2003, investment under the purview of local government increased 41.5 per cent, while central government projects actually decreased nearly 8 per cent. By 2003, following an extremely rapid increase in investment, especially in the housing market, a bubble economy began to form.

The central government began to take action only in June 2003. Between then and the end of the year, it issued instructions to the banks to restrict lending to the real estate sector, and sharply curtailed permission to the local governments to set up new development zones, the prime vehicle for investment in real estate by the provincial and local governments. It also raised the deposit reserve ratio[6]—the minimum that the banks had to have on deposit with the Central Bank, from 6 to 7 per cent—thereby reducing the amount that the banks could lend. Perhaps most important of all, it once again resorted to 'informal window guidance' that is physical control, to slowdown the expansion of credit (Naughton 2004a). Initially, these measures had little effect, for investment grew by 48 per cent in the first quarter of 2004 (World Bank 2004). Only in the second and third quarters, when the government began to ration credit to the steel, cement and other industries and where it saw excess capacity developing, did the growth of investment slowdown to between 20 and 30 per cent. The growth of value added in industry also moderated from 14.2 per cent in the fourth quarter of 2003 to 10.9 per cent in the first 9 months of 2004 (World Bank 2004).

But the slowdown did not last. Bank lending to industry and construction continued to skyrocket, forcing the Central Bank to raise the cash reserve ratio six times between June 2006 and April 2007 from 7 to 10.5 per cent. Despite this, total fixed investment, which had risen by 26 per cent in 2005 over 2004, shot up by another 24 per cent in 2006 (Sugiyama 2007).

Another increase was on the cards for 2007, because in January and February, bank credit grew by 37 per cent over the same period of the previous year and at twice the average rate recorded in 2006 (Huang and Cai 2007). Not surprisingly, in 2006, China's GDP grew by 10.7 per cent, a full 2.7 per cent more than the central government had planned for, and the highest growth that China had recorded in 11 years. Goldman Sachs predicted an even higher growth of 10.8 per cent in 2007 (Huang 2007).

One area in which the government was particularly keen to curb investment was real estate. Not only had this seen the biggest investment bubble develop between 1991 and 1996, but investment in real estate gobbled up land, which was being appropriated from the peasant at purely arbitrary, often token rates of compensation. As a result in 2003 and 2004, the central government gave specific instructions to the banks to put ceilings on loans to the real estate sector. Despite this, since Chinese cities continued to expand relentlessly, real estate projects did not lose their allure for the local authorities. In the first half of 2006, despite the curbs on lending for real estate projects, investment in them increased by 22 per cent over the second half of 2005 (Goodman 2006). In 2005 and 2006, therefore, despite every effort to check investment in land and real estate, a housing bubble had begun to develop yet again. This came abruptly to light in 2008 when housing sales fell 40 per cent in the first 9 months, compared to the previous year. The resulting collapse of demand for steel has forced one brand new giant steel plant, built at a cost of 28 billion yuan to stop production altogether (Barboza 2008).

The similarity between what was happening since 2002 and what had happened in the early 1990s was unmistakable, but it did not stop with the rates of growth, investment and bank credit. There was a similar build-up of unsold stocks across most of industry. In November 2006, the World Bank's Beijing office reported that unsold inventories had exceeded 15 per cent of output in a quarter of the 39 industrial sectors, as early as the first half of 2004. In the automobile industry, inventories amounted to 48 per cent of production.[7]

Chinese analysts persisted in regarding inflation as the prime danger arising from this runaway investment. 'Investment in assets is excessive, and there is an oversupply of loans', a spokesman for China's National Bureau of Statistics, Zheng Jingping, said at a news conference. 'In the long run, these will cause inflation. The government will be on guard for inflationary pressures' (Goodman 2006). Analysts for several international investment firms echoed this sentiment, but added that since China's inflation was still relatively moderate, especially in comparison to the early 1990s, there was no immediate risk of a crash landing for the economy. Both groups remained oblivious to the real significance of the renewed hyper-investment. This was the unambiguous demonstration of Beijing's failure to establish control over the economy through its reform of economic policy and decision-making structures within the government. As had happened in the 1980s and early 1990s, the provincial authorities had once again run away with the bit between their teeth. And it is Beijing that will once again have to clean up the mess.

7

An Ancient Struggle in a New Guise

The central government's failure to control the third surge in investment that began in 2002 gives striking proof of its lack of control over the economy. The reasons are not economic but political. The key to understanding this is to be found in the anomaly of the Chinese economic transformation that was described above. Most of the excess capacity that is responsible for China's wasteful growth and its fragile financial health is not a legacy of the communist era. It was created in the 1980s and 1990s, after the move to a market economy had already begun. And most of it resulted not from private investment but fresh investment by the state.

Minxin Pei attributes the investment spree by the local governments to Beijing's decision to adopt 'a unique form of fiscal decentralisation' (Pei 2006). This made local governments responsible for collecting taxes from the enterprises in their jurisdiction. The 'tax contracting' system that developed between 1980 and 1983 allowed them to tax the enterprises not only on their own account but also on behalf of the central government. Since the local governments and the enterprises shared a common desire to retain as much of the surpluses generated by the latter for themselves, they were able to find a dozen of ways of minimizing the amount that they had to hand over to Beijing, thereby maximizing the amount they kept for themselves.

But the changes of policy between 1981 and 1983 went far beyond fiscal devolution. As Beijing reduced the scope of centralized planning and distribution, party cadres, township, city and provincial administrators and enterprise managers, all became 'investors'. In this, they encountered absolutely no check from the Banking system, because bank officials in the local branches were subordinated by law to the local party committee at their level of government and in particular to the Party Secretary. The result was a huge burst of investment in the 1980s, which was cut short only by the draconian measures against inflation that the Peoples' Bank of China took in 1988 to contain inflation, and the sharp 2-year recession that followed.

The recession did not last long. In the coastal provinces, in particular, the provincial and city administrations had tasted blood, and were champing at the bit to resume investment. Deng Xiaoping's 'retirement' to Shanghai during the conservative backlash that followed the Tiananmen uprising, his southern tour in 1992 and his endorsement of the 'socialist market economy' took all remaining restraints off the new 'cadre capitalists'. Beginning in 1991 they literally ran away with investment. But these cadre capitalists became a unique type of investor—one with unlimited funds at their disposal and free from personal risk of failure in case the investment went sour. Most of the new enterprises were created at various levels of the local government. By the time it was over, there was severe excess capacity in 80 per cent of the products of Chinese industry. An estimated 70 per cent of the office and residential space, created during the boom years also failed to find any buyers despite several reduction in prices and rents in 1997 and 1998 (OECD 2000: 134).

From Communism to Cadre Capitalism

The motives that drove the burst of investment in the state-owned enterprises (SOEs) and the 'non-state', collective enterprises in the 1980s and 1990s were varied. Fiscal decentralization and a progressive reduction of the planned sector gave the provincial, city, district and township authorities the opportunity to decide their own investments. This set off a race between provinces and, within them, between prefectures, counties and townships, to outdo each other in finding new ways of meeting and exceeding targets, for that was one sure way for party cadres to climb within the hierarchy of the administration and the Chinese Communist Party (CCP) (Nee and Peng 1994).

Greater autonomy also gave rise to the temptation to use their control of the supply of factors of production and key raw materials to make money, personally out of their deployment. As is described in the next chapter, the ways of doing so were literally endless. These motives, the personal and the institutional, fused to create a powerful urge in the local and provincial administrations to appropriate the development and liberalization agenda. In the long run, this turned out to be a mixed blessing because while it was responsible for the dazzling acceleration of growth in output, incomes and exports, between 1984 and 1995, it also resulted in Beijing's loss of control over investment and consequently, the boom and bust cycles that China has experienced and may experience again in the near future.

The local cadres used three instruments that they controlled. These were their control over taxation to raise the seed money for the new investment, their control (and later influence) over local banking officials to compel them to give the necessary loans and their power to provide the land needed for new industrial ventures to sprout upon.

The cause of industrial duplication is therefore not economic but political. China's hectic and resource-intensive growth has been the product of an unacknowledged struggle between the central leadership and cadres of the government and Communist Party and its local cadres to control and deploy the productive resources of the state—land, capital and labour. Since the mid-1980s, power has swung back and forth between them like a see-saw—into the hands of local government in the 1980s, wrested back savagely in 1989 and 1990; back to the provinces and local governments in 1991, seized again by Beijing through its 1994 tax reforms and yet again by the 1998 centralization of control over bank credit, and somewhat inexplicably, lost once more to the local and provincial authorities after 2002. President Hu Jintao's 2006 decision to abolish all agricultural taxes and fees levied on farmers was the latest salvo in this seemingly unending battle.

An Ancient Struggle in a New Guise

Could Beijing not have foreseen what would happen if it devolved all the components of economic decision-making power to the local governments? A growing number of authors have concluded that it did not cede powers voluntarily; but had these wrested from them by the local governments. What is more, this process did not begin after the first reforms—those of land cultivation rights—were formally announced in 1979 but some years earlier, at the tail end of the Cultural Revolution. The local cadres began to disobey central diktats piecemeal in order to cope with pressing local problems that Beijing either was not aware of or was not able to address. But behind their readiness to 'interpret' the directives from the centre lay a decline of faith in its sagacity and respect for its authority. The reforms did not, therefore, emerge from the centre's strength but from its growing weakness in relation to the local cadres.[1]

Beijing lost a good deal of its hegemony over the local cadres because of the succession of radical but ill-conceived experiments that Mao launched as he faced the progressive failure of central planning to meet the needs and aspirations of the people. The hardships these inflicted on the people and the waste of lives that resulted sapped the unquestioning the people had in the central government and leadership. This emboldened peasants and local cadres to experiment with better ways of meeting their needs and obligations. But the local cadres might not have mustered up the courage to break the rules even then had provinces like Anhui and Szechuan, which were later hailed as 'pioneer provinces' in agricultural reform, not been hit by a succession of natural disasters in 1977–79 that forced their village cadres to choose between innovation and famine (Li 2002).

According to Lynn White, economic reform started in the early 1970s, when the violence of the Cultural Revolution had ended. Local networks—coalitions of local officials and managers—began to promote the development of rural industry. This proved a blessing in disguise because it relieved local shortages that were a regular by-product of the miscalculations of centralized planning. The centre therefore tolerated it and may even have tacitly encouraged it. But over time it undermined the rationale for centralized planning by showing that decentralized production could meet changing consumption needs much better than the cumbersome central plan machinery. It also initiated the competition for resources and control of output between the central and local cadres in government. The diversion of an increasing share of economic activity from central to local control began to erode the revenues and increase the financial burdens on the central government. As this gained momentum during the mid-1970s and late 1970s, central leaders were forced to accept and attempt to streamline the changes that had already begun.

Dali Yang traced the economic assertiveness of peasants and rural cadres even further back to the catastrophic failure of the Great Leap Forward campaign, in the late 1950s. The famine and deaths led to a return to family farming in some areas in the early 1960s. But this was nipped in the bud by a fresh bout of radicalism during the Cultural Revolution and a spate of new hardships on the peasants. This left both peasants and local officials disillusioned with and distrustful of central directives. When the political climate changed after Mao's death, peasants and local cadres took the lead in restructuring their economic relations with the state. This created a groundswell that compelled the central leadership to de-collectivize agriculture in the early 1980s.

Daniel Kelliher concurred with White that the earliest reforms— that is, de-collectivization, commercialization and the rise of a private economy in agriculture—were all initiated by peasants rather than the state. Motivated by the desire to escape their economic plight, they went beyond the limits set by central leaders to change the commune system. But although the rural cadres took the initiative, they were able to continue experimenting with reforms because they had, or soon acquired, the tacit consent of the state. The economic alternatives that they pursued, such as family farming, led to such sharp increases in output that they also had the unforeseen effect of meeting the grain delivery quotas and other policy imperatives of the state, better than the communes had done before. As a consequence, central leaders gave a somewhat grudging recognition to what peasants innovated (Shao 2006).[2]

Another reform that also occurred in spite, rather than because, of, directives from Beijing was the relaxation of controls on migration by villagers to the towns. This too was initiated by local authorities who set up township industries well before 1978. It too was initially opposed by the central leadership. In fact, the centre lifted the ban on rural–urban migration only in 1988, when the migrant workers had already become an indispensable part of the booming industrial economy (Li 2002).

The assertiveness of local cadres was not the only reason for the initiation of reforms. The desire to make a break with the policies of the past was also strong in party cadres at higher levels, because many of them had suffered during the Cultural Revolution. It was also supported by hundreds of thousands of young people who had been sent into the countryside and seen the miserable conditions in which the peasants lived. These were inducted into the universities in large numbers in the late 1970s on their return, and came out of them imbued with a desire for change. Thus, when the central government legitimized the Household Responsibility System, thereby formalizing the dissolution of the communes allowed enterprises to retain their post-tax surpluses and decentralized the fiscal system, it took the lid of a pressure cooker that had been coming to a boil for some time.

The Struggle to Control Investment

The duplication of new productive facilities was not based upon any plan or design developed by, or in concert with, Beijing, but was the direct result of the competition between the central and local cadres to monopolise investment.

This massive duplication of industrial facilities is revealed by the similarity of industrial structures created in each of the provinces. In 1989 the industrial structure of 22 out of China's 34 provinces was 90 per cent, identical to that of China taken as a whole. In 1994, it was 90 per cent identical in 13 provinces and 80 per cent identical in 21. Seven years later, 23 provinces manufactured washing machines, 29 made television sets, another 23 made washing machines and no fewer than 27 assembled automobiles. In the mid-1990s, among the 39 industrial sectors, the largest eight firms accounted for less than 10 per cent of the market share in 18 sectors (Pei 2006: 126). The Table 7.1 reveals the impact this has had on China's industrial structure:

Table 7.1: International Comparison of the Enterprise or Facility in Energy Intensive Industry (2004)

Category	China	Foreign
Coal Mines	28,000 with average annual output of 70,000 tonnes	9 in Germany, average annual output of 5.56 million tonnes
Refineries	56 with annual processing capacity of 4.19 million tonnes	6 in South Korea, annual processing capacity of 21.47 million tonnes
Blast Furnaces	263 with average annual steel production of 750,000 tonnes	29 in Japan, annual steel production of 2.83 million tonnes
Cement Factories	5,027 with an average annual output of 190,000 tonnes	65 in Japan, average annual output of 1.14 million tonnes

Source: Qingyi 2006.

Even the 5,000 cement plants in 2004 was an improvement over the situation that had existed earlier. According to the OECD, in 1996 there were then 8,000 cement plants in China as against 110 in the United States, 51 in Russia, 58 in Brazil and 106 in India (OECD 2000: 15).

Every industry thus has a core of reasonably modern and efficient companies surrounded by a large penumbra of loss-making, inefficient enterprises. In 1999, 15 out of 115 automobile companies accounted for 1.155 million , or 87 per cent of the output of cars. The reminder produced anything from zero to a few thousand cars. In 2000, the steel industry had 1,570 independent companies, of which only four manufactured more than 5 million tonnes a year and another 27 produced a million tonnes each. In 1997, the government announced a massive restructuring plan by which loss-making companies would be merged with profitable ones, to create four large enterprises that would produce 40 per cent of the national output (OECD 2000: 177–78). But as the above table shows, this has only partially resolved the problem of small size and obsolete technology.

In 1999, 25 major industrial product groups of the largest eight firms together produced only 12.2 per cent of the output. This was a marginal improvement over their 11.7 per cent share in 1990. In nine of them, the share of the largest eight firms had actually declined. The negligible increase in consolidation of output shows, how little the fate of these enterprises depended upon the dictates of the market (OECD 2000: 167). For while the decision to establish these enterprises was taken by the local authorities in competition with Beijing, once they were up and running, the local governments were as reluctant to close them down and take over the burden of compensating the laid-off workers as the central government (OECD 2000).

The excess of productive capacity inevitably led to overproduction, mounting inventories of unsold goods, and a steep increase in the losses of the SOEs. In March 1997, the *China Business Review*, the Washington-based journal of the US–China Business Council, reported a World Bank estimate that 17 per cent of China's GDP consists of 'unsaleable' SOE-manufactured goods.[3] China's State Statistics Bureau estimated that in the first 11 months of 1996, the losses of the loss-making SOEs increased by 43.6 per cent over the previous year, to an estimated $6.4 billion at the end of November; the earnings of profitable SOEs also declined by 49.3 per cent to $5.9 billion. As recession strengthened its grip on the Chinese economy, the losses mounted. *Xinhua* reported that losses at the

SOEs more than tripled in October and November and a Beijing economist told the *South China Morning Post* that the December figures were likely to be even worse.[4] In November 2004, an article in the *Peoples' Daily*, which extolled China's success in surmounting the crisis of profitability, conveniently blamed upon the Asian financial crisis, admitted that in 1997, 160,000 SOEs had been running at a loss. Restructuring had been responsible for bringing the number down to 74,000 by the end of 2003 (*Peoples' Daily* 2004). Like many other Chinese first estimates, these are somewhat dubious, but they clearly indicate the direction in which the Chinese economy was heading in 1996.

This uncontrolled investment, which has led periodically to huge build ups of excess capacity in most industries, explains the paradox of China's great efficiency in the production of goods and simultaneous inefficiency in consumption of raw materials and energy. The resulting waste of industrial inputs, including energy, was more than evident when on the occasion of finalizing the 11th Plan it was mentioned that China is consuming six times more raw materials than the US and three times more than India to produce the same value of goods. As was mentioned earlier, with one-tenth of the world's GDP in terms of purchasing power, China is consuming between one-third and one-sixth of the worlds traded raw materials. This includes a third of its coal and one-eights of its total energy. With 2.3 times India's PPP–GDP, China consumes seven to 20 times as much of every important primary raw material that enters world trade. These trends cannot be sustained indefinitely.

The Struggle to Control Markets

Burdened with excess capacity, and squeezed by recession after 1995, the provincial administrations resorted to the only other means at hand to keep their enterprises running profitably. This was to keep rival products made in other provinces out of their provincial markets. Several scholars believe that local protectionism did not exist before 1978 (Pei 2006: 126). If this is indeed so then its rapid rise during the reform era provides additional proof that reform drastically weakened the authority of Beijing over the provincial governments.

Local protectionism took the form of a variety of administrative and fiscal barriers to trade with other provinces. Some of these were legal: others were not. These included quantitative restrictions, a variety of regulatory hurdles, such as health and trade mark inspections, and various 'fees' that enterprises wanting to 'export' their products to another province had to pay, which were nothing but a novel form of import duty. In 1998, the fees levied by various provinces on automobile sales amounted to 160 billion yuan, of which half was estimated to be illegal. In that year, the total net profit of the automobile industry was only 4 billion yuan. In 2001, 18 provinces had passed laws that either banned or imposed a ceiling on the sale of liquor made in other provinces. A survey of 3,539 enterprise managers all over the country, by the Development Research Centre of the central government in 2002, showed that all provinces practised local protectionism, and that it was as prevalent in the less-developed central provinces as in the industrially advanced coastal provinces (Pei 2006: 127).

Indirect but compelling evidence of this comes from the fact that between 1985 and 1992, China's exports grew by 17 per cent and its imports by 10 per cent a year and its annual domestic retail sales by 9 per cent, but its inter-province trade grew by only 4.2 per cent a year (Pei 2006: 128). The entire economy was therefore 'turning outwards'. But the coastal provinces led the way. And as their income and wealth became less and less dependent upon their economic ties with the rest of the country, their ability to ignore or deflect Beijing's directives and set up competing economic systems increased.

The Struggle over Taxation

Nothing reveals the competition between the central government and the local administrations in China as unequivocally as the tug of war that the two have waged to capture the financial resources of the state. The struggle began soon after Beijing adopted a series of tax reforms between 1980 and 1983, as it began the transition to a market-guided economy. The purpose of the reforms was to stimulate entrepreneurship in the SOEs by shifting from a Soviet style to a modern taxation system that left control of post-tax profits in the hands of those who earned them. Under the new system, designated the fiscal contracting system, the enterprises had to pay a tax on their operating surpluses, fixed by the centre but collected by the city and provincial governments. The latter then bargained with the centre to determine how much of the tax they would pass on to it.

The 'fiscal contracting' system created a powerful incentive for the enterprises to conceal as much as possible of their surpluses from the city and provincial authorities, and for the latter to do the same with respect to the central government. This had two deleterious effects on central revenues. The first was to reduce their buoyancy and the second was to reduce their share of total revenues, in relation to the provinces. Buoyancy fell from a not too satisfactory 0.78, between 1978 and 1985 (one per cent increase in GDP at current prices led to a 0.78 per cent increase in tax revenues) to 0.53, between 1985 and 1993 (Bahl 1999). This resulted in a steep decline in the centre's revenues, from 35 per cent in 1978 to 10.7 per cent of GDP in 1993 and severely curtailed its capacity to take over the welfare obligations of the SOEs and give them a chance to compete successfully against the non-state sector in the increasingly competitive market for products. In 1990, central expenditures were running 10 per cent ahead of revenue. This rose to 23 per cent on an average, between 1995 and 2000. In 2000, the fiscal deficit amounted to 4.55 per cent of the GDP. A growing part was being used to finance current consumption (Holz and Zhu 2002: 72, Table 3).

Even as the ratio of central taxes to GDP declined, there was a parallel accumulation of funds in the hands of the enterprises and the provincial and city authorities amounting, according to one IMF estimate, to 14.5 per cent of the GDP in 1992 (Arora and Norregaard 1997: Table 2).[5] The overall effect of the fiscal contracting system was not so much to reduce total government revenue as to divert a large part of it from the central government to the provincial authorities. Table 7.2 shows the impact of the fiscal contracting system and the subsequent efforts by the central government to recapture a larger share of the tax revenues. In 1985, the revenue and expenditure of both the central and the local governments were more or less balanced. But by 1993, the centre's share of total revenues had fallen from 38.4 per cent to a mere 22 per cent. That of the provinces and municipalities had increased from 61.6 to 78 per cent. The central government therefore plunged into deficit.

In 1994, the central government passed a tax reform law that replaced fiscal contracting with a 'tax sharing' system that sharply wrested control of finances back from the local authorities. Its purpose

Table 7.2: Central and Local Shares of Revenue and Expenditure 1985–2004

Year	Central		Local	
	Revenue	Expenditure	Revenue	Expenditure
1985	38.4	39.7	61.6	60.3
1993	22	28.3	78	71.7
1994	55.7	30.3	44.3	69.7
1998	49.5	28.9	50.5	71.1
2004	54.9	27.7	45.1	72.3

Source: *China Statistical Yearbook* 2006.

was to raise the share of central revenues in the total to 60 per cent, a goal that it came close to achieving because its share of tax revenues rose to 55.7 per cent in 1994, the first year after the reform. The local authorities' share of revenues crashed from 78 to 44.3 per cent (Ong 2006). However, while the centre reduced the share of the provinces' tax, it did not reduce their expenditure commitments. As a result in 1994, while Beijing had a revenue surplus amounting to 25.4 per cent of total tax revenues, the provinces went into deficit to the same extent. This gap was never filled. After a small recovery to 50.5 per cent in 1998, provincial revenues fell back again to 45.1 per cent in 2004. Its expenditure, however, rose to 72.3 per cent. So the budgetary gap increased to 27.3 per cent in 2004.

The expenditure gap that opened was to be filled by transfers of money from the central government and by economies in their administrative and other expenditures. The economies never occurred, so although the 'tax transfers' met 17 per cent of the local authorities' expenses, they did not suffice to close the gap between expenditure and revenue. The mismatch of revenues and expenditure was particularly stark at the county and township levels, where the local authorities were expected to meet both health and education expenses. That the central government's purpose was not to allocate better resources but to wrest back financial power back from the provinces was apparent from the fact that while it reduced their revenue, it actually increased their expenditure obligations, by making them responsible for the full 9 years of schooling for children.

The local authorities responded by increasing tax levies and extracting a number of 'fees' and 'contributions' from local enterprises and peasants. The centre put a stop to this, however, in 1998 by implementing another reform which came to be dubbed the tax-for-fees policy. But this made the townships and counties bear down harder on the peasants. The total extra-budgetary revenues collected at sub-national levels therefore jumped from 53.2 billion yuan in 1982 to 315.5 billion yuan in 1999 (Yep 2004).

The township and county authorities also sought to bridge the gap by going into debt. In all, they incurred five types of debt. They borrowed directly from the ministry of finance, the Central Bank, international institutions and foreign investors; they ran up arrears of payment to their staff and deferred payment for the goods they bought, such as grain from the peasants; they borrowed through local financial institutions that they controlled to meet their current expenditure on public services and the infrastructure. They floated informal credit institutions called Rural Credit Foundations and borrowed from them; and they floated new enterprises with loans that they guaranteed, although the budget law expressly forbade them from doing so (Yep 2004). After 1998, their plight became so serious that a study carried out in 2004 by two Chinese scholars, Tian Fa and Chenying Zhou, showed that the combined debt of the county, township and village administrations in 2003 had reached 1 trillion yuan, or 8.3 per cent of the GDP (Ong 2006).

The Struggle to Control Bank Lending

As was described in Chapter 3, there was a similar struggle over access to bank lending. Till 1998, local authorities had taken advantage of the subordination of the officials of the local branches of the state-owned commercial banks to the local party committee to virtually dictate the loans they wanted. To access the loans, they had set up a large network of trusts and holding companies and quasi-banking institutions. In October 1997, the Central Committee and the State Council jointly issued a 'Notice concerning deepening financial reform, rectifying financial order and preventing financial risk'. At one stroke of the pen, it removed local branches of the state banks and the Peoples' Bank of China from the local party committees' jurisdiction and placed them under a newly formed Central Finance Work Committee. It also wound up hundreds of locally controlled trust and investment companies and underground banks. But the struggle has continued and as the central government's failure to control the investment spree indulged in by the local authorities in 2003–07 shows, the latter have found a variety of ways to get around Beijing's diktat.

Trading in Land

But the local governments' most spectacular and most socially damaging foray was into the marketizing of land. When, following the success of the original four Special Economic Zones, the central government permitted the other provinces to set up similar zones, a kind of land grab frenzy developed, in which provincial, city and prefecture authorities all participated with abandon. Between 1988 and 1993, they set up 6,000 development zones, covering a total of 15,000 sq.km. This was 1,600 sq.km more than the entire urban area of the country in 1993. In total, four-fifths of his land was arable land taken away from the farmers by virtue of their lack of individual title to it. In Guangdong province, the land taken out of cultivation, amounted to half of all the arable land in the province. In addition to this, there were so-called 'enclosed zones'—development zones that had been carved out by the township and village-level administrations, for setting up township and village enterprises. No one had any precise estimate of how much land these had swallowed (Qinliang 2000b).

The enclosure movement, for that is indeed what it was, was very largely speculative. None of the concerned authorities knew, for certain, which enterprises intended to move there and from where. This was 'blind development' and it met the expected fate. A majority of the development zones never took off. But the land remained enclosed and fallow for the next decade and a half, till in 2005, under President Hu Jintao, 4,755 of them were disbanded and the land returned to the communes. These mounted to 70.1 per cent of all the development zones that had been set up till then.

Despite this, since Chinese cities continue to expand relentlessly, real estate projects have not lost their allure for the local authorities. In the first half of 2006, despite the curbs on lending for real estate projects that the central government had instituted, investment in them increased by 22 per cent, over the second half of 2005 (Goodman 2006). In 2005 and 2006, therefore, despite every effort to check investment in land and real estate, a bubble economy developed yet again.

8

Recession and the Birth of Class Conflict

The competition that developed between the central and local governments and the corresponding cadres of the Communist Party explains several perplexing features of China's enigma-ridden growth. It accounts for China's phenomenal rate of growth. But it also explains why it has been so uneven, why it is so heavily biased towards investment and why it is so prodigiously wasteful in its consumption of raw materials and energy. This competition did not force the pace of privatization but overwhelmed it. Suddenly, the *Getihu*[1] and the technocrat managers, who were China's first truly private entrepreneurs, were shoved aside by more than 47,000 pseudo-entrepreneurs (Bahl and Martinez-Vazquez 2003), variously referred to by Chinese scholars as cadre or *nomenklatura* capitalists, with virtually limitless access to finance and free from the burden of entrepreneurial risk. It was an investors' paradise, and they went stamping in with a verve and abandon, that has never been seen before.

These new entrepreneurs developed management skills and market knowledge at a phenomenal rate. They were the first to become aware of the legal and institutional changes that needed to be made. Themselves being the government, they were able to make the required changes with a celerity that foreign investors had seldom encountered elsewhere. It is not surprising therefore, that when wage rates began to climb in east and south-east Asia, China became the favoured destination of enterprises looking for an offshore manufacturing platform from where to continue their penetration of the global market.

So long as the investment made by the 'cadre capitalists' of the local governments was subject to the discipline of the international market and the foreign collaborators, this arrangement proved phenomenally successful. But all its drawbacks became apparent in the domestic market, where these constraints were notably absent. With no central planning, and none of the discipline of the market, the Chinese economy became a runaway horse without reigns. When one enterprise in one province sensed a new market opportunity or found a new niche in the global or domestic market, scores of other enterprises in other provinces and cities rushed into it in the pioneer's wake. This is the cause of China's short and violent trade cycles—its rapid transitions from shortage to glut, from profit to loss and from plenitude to poverty, in the financial fortunes of the township and village enterprises.

This unique form of growth—driven by the anticipation of profit but without the consonant risk of loss—has imposed immense strain on the social system and created a series of threats to the political stability and legitimacy of the state. First, as has happened in all other early capitalist economies, rapid growth has increased differences in income and wealth. According to the Chinese Academy of Social Sciences, The Gini coefficient rose to 0.496 in 2006, from 0.47 in 2005, making China one of the half dozen most inegalitarian societies in the world (Cai 2006). Second, the unevenness of growth has increased the stress of adjustment upon society. The sharp booms of 1985–89 and 1991–95 have led to rapid increases in employment and income that have been reversed in the recessions that have followed, in 1989–91 and 1996–2001. Since the rich have a greater capacity to resist impoverishment in periods of economic contraction, the poor have had to bear a disproportionate share of the hardship that they have caused. The boom that began in 2002 is almost certain to be followed by another sharp recession. When that happens, the poor are likely, once more, to bear the lion's share of the pain.

Third, and most serious, corruption has been the Siamese twin of this cadre-led growth. Bribery, kickbacks, fraud and embezzlement have become inseparable from investment, but these are only a part of the story. The 'cadre capitalists' of the non-state sector differ from their genuine counterparts in market societies in one crucially important way: they can enrich themselves either by making profits or by extracting 'rent'. They have done both. Bribery, fraud and embezzlement have become commonplace. But opportunities for practicing these are restricted to the select few. For the vast majority of the cadres, there has been the exploitation of their bureaucratic and, less often, their judicial power to extract money in exchange for administrative sanction. During periods of rapid growth, profits have been the cadres' main source of income, most of which has been extracted as increases in salary and perquisites. But in the downward phase of the trade cycle, when profits have disappeared, they have used their political power to safeguard their incomes and perquisites by treating them as fixed costs. Thus, while China's poor could have accepted the polarization of income and wealth and the stress caused by sharp economic expansions and contractions as unavoidable consequences of embracing the 'socialist market economy', that is capitalism, the systematic abuse of political and bureaucratic power by the party cadres to enrich themselves at the expense of the people has aroused their anger and endangered the stability of the political system.

Power, Corruption and Extortion

The struggle between the central and local party cadres for control over investable resources remained dormant during the second half of the 1980s and the first half of the 1990s, because the Chinese economy grew at well over 10 per cent per annum. Since the pie was growing rapidly, there was enough for everyone and the recession of 1989–90 was too short to change peoples' perceptions. For the same reason, there was also little sign of the discontent among workers and peasants that was to surface at the end of the 1990s. In 1993, at the end of what might well come to be recalled as the Age of Contentment, there were only 8,700 public expressions of popular discontent and nearly all involved only a handful of persons. But the situation changed radically when the rebound from the overinvestment of the previous decade led to recession in the second half of the 1990s. Recession sharpened the struggle for the control of capital between the central and local strata of the party, between the controllers of capital and the emerging underclass of workers and peasants. As a result in 2005, when Prime Minister Wen Jiabao sounded the alarm, the number had climbed to 87,000.

Recession replaced a sellers' market with a buyers' market. The resulting decline in prices and accumulation of unsold stocks killed whatever chance the old state-owned enterprises (SOEs) had had of adjusting to the new, competitive environment. What is more, it also pushed thousands of the newly established SOEs, and millions of hastily created, urban collectives and TVEs into insolvency and had to be 'wound up' in one way or another.

The stress this caused was not felt by the 'cadre capitalists' who had sanctioned the investment, but by the workers and peasants whom they employed or oversaw. As the off-account profits of the small and medium-sized SOEs that had been turned over to the local governments declined or turned into losses, and as TVE profits fell and losses mounted, the revenues of the local administration declined. With no reduction in the duties assigned to them by the central government, and no desire to cut their 'non-developmental' spending upon salaries, perquisites, new office buildings, automobiles, entertainment and travel, the township administrations were left with no option but to squeeze the peasants and local enterprises ever harder to extract the funds they needed. So they resorted to delays in payments of pensions, stipends for laid-off workers and health expenditure reimbursements for urban workers and unemployed, and to ever heavier extortions of money as *ad hoc* fees, taxes and dues from the peasants.

Towards Insolvency

The financial pressure that the SOEs came under can be gauged from their profits and losses and the ratio of the first to the second during the 1990s.

Table 8.1: Total Profits Earned by Profit-making Firms and Losses of the Loss-makers, between 1991 and 2000 (in billions of yuan)

Year	1990	1991	1992	1993	1994	1995	1996	1997	1998*	1999*	2000*
Profit	73.7	76.9	90.4	127.0	131.1	130.4	120.3	125.3	154.8	184.8	302.3
Loss	34.9	36.7	36.9	45.3	48.3	69.0	79.1	83.1	102.3	99.8	61.6
Ratio	2.1	2.1	2.4	2.8	2.7	2.0	1.5	1.5	1.5	2.2	4.9

Source: Carten Holz and Tian Zhu 2002.

Note: *The absolute figures for profit and loss in these years are not comparable with those for the earlier years because the category 'SOEs' was replaced by 'SOEs and state-controlled shareholding companies'.

The profits of the profit-making companies rose rapidly from 1990 till 1993, but their growth slowed down in 1994—an early warning of the recession that was to come—and then declined in absolute terms from 1995 till 1998. The losses too were low till 1994, but began to rise sharply after that and stayed high till 1999. They began to fall only in 2000 when the recession bottomed out and a recovery set in. More revealing than the absolute figures, however, is the ratio of profit to loss within the state-owned sector. This rose steadily during the boom years from 2.1 in 1990 and 1991 to 2.8 in 1993 and 2.7 in 1994. The decline in this ratio to 2.0 in 1995 was an early indication that Chinese industry had begun to suffer the consequences of its investment spree and was having some difficulty in selling its products. Thereafter, as recession set in, it declined to 1.5 in 1996, 1997 and 1998 before rising once more to 2.2 in 1999 and 4.91 in 2000, as recovery had set in (Holz and Zhu 2002: 78, Table 2).

The non-state enterprises did not fare any better. A tabulation for 165,080 state and non-state enterprises above a designated size, given a newly created database in the *China Statistical Yearbook* (CSY) 2005, shows that this ratio was 1.83 in 1998, but rose to over 10 to 1 in 2004 and 9 to 1 in 2005, when the Chinese economy entered a boom, and showed signs of overheating (CSY 2006: Table 13.5).[2]

Retrenchment and Unemployment

Privatization, or the transfer of enterprises from the state sector to the non-state sector, was accompanied by a large-scale retrenchment of workers. Employment in the state sector declined from a peak of 112.6 million in 1995 to 64.8 million in 2005 (CSY 2005: Table 5.10).[3] Another 28 million were laid off by the urban collectives between 1991 and 2005 (Giles et al. 2006). However, till 2000, most of this reduction was achieved by transferring the workers, along with their enterprises to the non-state sector. After adjusting for this, and for definitional changes in 1998, when laid-off (*xiagang*) workers ceased to be counted as employed, layoffs reduced total manufacturing employment by around 9.13 million between 1997 and 2002 (Bannister 2005).

In 1997, the Jiang Zemin/Zhu Rongji government announced its intention to embark upon a sustained programme of restructuring and followed this up, a few months later, with a 3-year programme to reduce the workforce in the SOEs. But the recession invalidated the basic premise upon which this programme was built—that 3 years would be sufficient for the laid-off workers to find alternate jobs in the non-state sector. For while the government was laying off workers from the SOEs, the recession was forcing a contraction in the non-state sector as well. The economy had therefore all but ceased to create new jobs. The Chinese government did not acknowledge this. Officially, there was an increase of 82.9 million urban jobs and a decline of 5.3 million jobs in the rural areas between 1995 and 2005 (CSY 2006: Table 5.1). Thus, 77.6 million new jobs were created in the decade after 1995. But this figure hides more than it reveals.

A closer examination of the employment data by sectors of employment shows a huge discrepancy between the overall figures and the sectoral data. The latter show that 71.2 million jobs were lost in this decade in the urban areas and 69.24 million created. Thus, despite the fact that China was at the height of another investment boom in 2005, there were 2 million fewer employed persons in 2005 than in 1995.

The rural areas, by contrast, saw a small *increase* in the employment of 18.5 million. Thus, there were 16.5 million more persons employed in 2005 than a decade previously. But, according to the National Bureau of Statistics, in the same period the economically active population increased from 688.5 to 778.7 million, an increase of 90.2 million. So where did the balance of 73.7 million persons go? The probable explanation is that most, if not all, are migrant workers—casual or seasonal labour—who are included neither in the urban nor in the rural tally, but are included in the total estimate of employment, which is obtained independently. A sample survey carried out by the National Bureau of Statistics showed that in 2005, the number of migrant workers who were holding down jobs in urban areas for more than 6 months in the year amounted to 145.8 million (CSY 2006: Table 4.9).[4] A decade earlier, the most commonly accepted figure for migrant labour, defined as those who lived outside their home counties for more than 200 days in a year, had been 80 million (World Bank 1997). The increase in their number over the last decade may account for the major part of discrepancy.

These figures are not reassuring. They suggest that all but a small proportion of the new entrants into the labour market after 1995 are entering it at the bottom, in jobs that are poorly paid, offer no security of employment and few, if any, social security benefits. There is no tally of migrant workers who work for less than 6 months a year in the urban areas. But 'urban unemployment (has) forced tens of millions of rural immigrants back to their home villages and police repression (has) failed to stem the rising tide of discontent' (Lewis and Litai 2003: 930). Tables 8.2 and 8.3 give the growth of employment in the urban and rural areas.

The Demise of the Workers' State

Among the SOEs, unemployment hit workers in the manufacturing industry especially hard. These workers accounted for 83 per cent of the total numbers laid-off.[5] To ease the pain of separation for the workers laid-off from the SOEs, the government enacted a new social security policy that came into force in 1998. Intended for permanent workers who were employed before the contract working system came into being in 1986, the new policy promised 60 per cent of the last salary drawn for a transitional period of 3 years. The workers laid-off under this scheme, called the off-post (*xiagang*) workers, were to retain their health and retirement benefits. While the official media claimed spectacular success for the policy, a detailed sample survey carried out by three researchers, in five large cities at the end of 2001, showed that the laid-off workers had suffered a considerable fall in their incomes even when they found jobs. They also faced modest wage and pension arrears and a steep fall in health benefits and high arrears of reimbursement for their expenses on health (Giles et al. 2006).

Out of all the deprivations, the one that caused the most anger in the workers was delay in the payment of pensions. In Benxi, a railroad, coal and steel industry city of just under 1 million in Liaoning, all but one of more than 20 protests was triggered by pension arrears. The lone exception was a sit in, in front of the city government office to demand subsidies for *xiagang* workers who had been denied all benefits (Hurst and O'Brien 2002: 346). Pensions take precedence over most other grievances because they are a symbolic recognition by the state and firm of an employee's years of devoted service as well as a vital source of support for those who are too old to work. One Benxi coal miner, who had been jobless for 10 years and had

Table 8.2: Changes in Urban Employment 1995–2005 (by main sectors)

Year	(Urban and Rural) Total	Urban Total	SOEs	Collectives	Limited Liability Companies	Share-Holding Companies	Private Companies	Hong Kong and Foreign Companies	Self-Employed
1995	680.65	190.40	112.61	31.47	—	1.64	6.20	5.13	17.09
2005	758.25	273.61	64.88	8.10	17.50	6.99	34.58	12.45	27.78
Change	+77.6	+82.9	−47.8	−23.4	+17.5	+5.35	+28.38	+7.32	+10.69

Table 8.3: Changes in Rural Employment 1995–2005 (by sectors)

Year	Total	TVEs	Private	Self-Employed
1995	490.25	128.62	4.71	30.54
2005	484.94	142.72	23.66	21.23
Change	−5.3	+14.1	+19	−9.3

Source for both tables: China Statistical Yearbook 2006.

not received any payments from her former firm or the state—neither wages nor *xiagang* benefits—and had lost any health insurance coverage she once had claim to, said that she would never consider demonstrating in order to obtain the *xiagang* benefits to which she was entitled but would protest with great resolve if, upon reaching retirement age, her pension were delayed or withheld (Hurst and O'Brien 2002: 350).

Other than pensions, the loss or delay of health care was the denial that workers most resented. The five-city study cited earlier revealed that health coverage had dropped by 12.9 per cent between 1996 and 2001. As a result, only 56 per cent of the urban population enjoyed health care. In three of the five cities, the ration was below 50 per cent. The reason for the drop in coverage was that very few of the new employers to whom the laid-off state workers went, offered health benefits. More than half reported that they were dissatisfied with their condition (Lewis and Litai 2003).

Overall, in 2000, the per capita income in the families of laid-off workers was about 55 per cent of the average income in the urban areas. In cities with dying industry, such as Changchun, in the northeast, this had fallen to only 26 per cent of their income before they were laid off (Pei 2006: 199).

In the face of these massive layoffs, when new jobs did not materialize in the non-state sector, the various provincial and prefectural governments quickly succumbed to the financial pressure. In 1998, only half of the laid-off workers received minimum employment benefits regularly. In Changchun, only 5 per cent felt that they could count on the government to solve their difficulties. And in Laoning, unemployment benefits met only 7 per cent of the laid-off workers' income (Pei 2006: 200). The workers were therefore thrown back on their past savings, and when these ran out, were forced to borrow from, or live off other members of their families.

The workers did not take their sudden loss of security and status passively. By one frequently cited estimate, there were as many as 60,000 protests by labourers in 1998, and if a report in the Far Eastern Economic Review is to be believed, as many as 100,000 the following year (Solinger 2003; Xueqin 2001). Throughout the 1990s, the Ministry of Labour tallied thousands of public gatherings, strikes, petitions and demonstrations each year and according to a trade union journal, 247 workers' demonstrations occurred in Henan during 1998 alone (Hurst and O'Brien 2002).

A report on the demonstrations in Henan in 1998, compiled by the Henan Federation of Trade Unions calculated that 55 per cent of the incidents in that province were centred on some combination of wage arrears, pensions and 'livelihood difficulties' and that a further 26 per cent were based on grievances involving 'poor labour relations' or 'illegal dismissals'.

A survey of Chinese and foreign newspapers from 1996 to April 2001 also offers a glimpse into the complaints that precipitate popular action. Of 62 working class protests reported in *People's Daily*, *Worker's Daily*, *The New York Times*, *The Washington Post* and *AP News Service*, virtually all of them concerned benefits for laid-off workers (29 per cent), wages (34 per cent) or pensions (42 per cent) (Hurst and O'Brien 2002: 346).

Among those who were able to get work, mostly younger laid-off workers below the age of 40, one-fifth reported that their financial condition was worse than before; almost half said they were dissatisfied or very dissatisfied with their condition in their new job. Those who did not find work were much worse off. Among them, 48 per cent were financially worse off and 83.2 per cent 'dissatisfied' or 'very dissatisfied' with employment conditions (Giles et al. 2006). Few, in short, had been able to find remunerative forms of self-employment. In a recession, this was hardly surprising.

After 2001, the number of workers laid-off from the SOEs began to decline. From 5.2 million in 2001 the number fell to 2.6 million in 2003 (Giles et al. 2006: 94). Thus, the worst of the restructuring had come to an end. But the problems of the workers did not end. For by 2001, they had begun to feel the full impact of the drastic reduction in the creation of new jobs. In 1998, half of the laid-off workers were able to find new jobs. In 1999, the ratio fell to 35 per cent. In 2000, it fell further to 26 per cent and in 2001 to a paltry 11 per cent (Pei 2006: 200). The restructuring that was begun with such optimism in 1998 has thus left a legacy of bitterness that haunts the Chinese State till this day. The workers captured this sentiment in a satire:

> In the 50s we helped people.
> In the 60s we criticized people.
> In the 70s we deceived people.
> In the 80s everybody hired everybody else.
> In the 90s we 'slaughter'[6] whoever we see. (Guidi and Chuntao 2004: Chapter 5)

Distress in the Provinces

Difficult as their plight might have been, urban registered workers were the least affected segment of the working population. There is less information on what happened in the late 1990s to the smaller state enterprises that had been left to the provincial governments, the hundred million plus migrant workers who held down full-time or part-time jobs in the cities or the millions employed in the TVEs, but a study of the privatization of 670 township enterprises, carried out in 15 randomly selected counties in two provinces, Zhejiang and Jiangsu (Lee and Roselle 2003), showed that there was a marked rise in the rate of privatization between 1993 and 1998. Township leaders privatized only 8 per cent of the firms under their control in 1993. In 1997 and 1998, when recession was at its height, and also when the central leadership had given the official green signal for privatization, this rose to 30 per cent (Lee and Roselle 2003: 988). However, whereas workers had welcomed privatization at its beginning, at the tail end of the economic boom, they became increasingly reluctant to invest their savings, even in the enterprises where they worked, as its economic prospects darkened. The OECD did a detailed study of the first experiment in the complete privatization of 210 small and medium enterprises in Zhucheng, a town in Shandong. In 1994, the workers willingly bought between two and five shares in the enterprises on payment of 1,000 yuan per share. But when profits began to flag, presumably because of the economic slowdown, many of them had second thoughts. Since the shares could not be sold to outsiders, most of them sold their shares to the managers or to others within the enterprise and managed to make a small profit (OECD 2003: 45).

As the recession deepened, and more and more of the small and medium-sized enterprises began to fail, the sales of their shares to the workers began to acquire a coercive tinge. In a similar sale 4 years later, when the recession was at its height, workers in a 700-employee plant had to be coerced into buying 5,000 yuan worth of shares each, with the threat that if they did not do so, they would lose their jobs and be denied all the benefits that they were entitled to. A hundred or so of them refused and resorted to one of the early collective actions of the post-reform period (Cai 2002b: 334).

Insider privatization was only one of the several ways that the local administrations employed to cope with the declining viability of the enterprises that they had set up during the boom years. Another was to encourage mergers and buyouts of weak enterprises by stronger non-state or private firms. This resulted in a dramatic decline in the number of enterprises.

Several field studies of TVEs in selected regions also showed that the recession had forced a large number to close down. Lynette Ong found that in one county in Sichuan province, where there had been 239 township enterprises in 1995, only 30 were left in 2003 (Ong 2006). This deepened the fiscal crisis of the township administrations. Most of the townships had set up TVEs, not only to generate employment but also to create an additional source of revenue, via the business tax, to finance their budgets. In the early 1990s, when China had hardly known a recession, the TVEs had not yet known failure on any significant scale. This had therefore seemed the right thing to do. As one township official told Ong:

> Many collective enterprises were developed out of a 'me-too' mentality and ready access to financial capital. There was no viable business model to start with no due diligence was conducted to ensure (that) market demand for the products existed. And many township administrations set up enterprises and built more factories simply because their counterparts in other towns were doing so. (Ong 2006)

When the 1994 tax reforms reduced the township administrations' revenues, they established rural credit foundations (RCFs)—informal banks totally under their control—to raise savings from the villagers by offering higher rates of interest. More than one-third of the loans that these local informal banks disbursed went to the township enterprises and one-sixth to various government agencies. Very little of these advances were ever recovered. In the second half of the 1990s, a large proportion, often the majority, of the township enterprises collapsed. This created a financial crisis: the RCFs in particular became insolvent, and had to be taken over by the central government. Since 70 per cent of the deposits made with the RCFs came from individual families, the failure of these banks meant that a large part of the cost of recession had finally to be borne by them (Ong 2006).

To minimize their losses, the townships accelerated the pace of privatization. As more and more units began to incur losses, the central and local governments had to choose between subsidizing them and cutting them loose. The serious fiscal crisis that enveloped all tiers of the local administration would in any case have made them look for ways to reduce the fiscal burden upon themselves. Handing their loss-making TVEs over to their workers and managers, who stood a better chance of turning them around than any outsider, was the best course open to them. The directives from the central leadership, in 1997 and 1998, gave this option the necessary legitimacy. Between 1993 and 2002, the number of SOEs decreased from 1,951,700 to 1,172,500 and the number of collective enterprises decreased from 5,156,500 to 1,885,900. In the same period of time, the number of registered private enterprises increased from 237,900 to 2,435,300 (Fewsmith 2004). The increase in the latter was a fraction of the decline in the former. While a majority of the loss-makers were no doubt folded into other enterprises, it is difficult to believe that many, perhaps several hundred thousands, did not simply stop functioning and get closed down.[7]

The way in which the recession darkened the futures of township enterprises is also reflected by the sale prices that they commanded when they were privatized. A detailed study of valuation and sale of 88 enterprises, which was part of the larger study of the privatization of 670 township enterprises mentioned earlier, showed that, while 33 firms had sold for 75 per cent to more than 100 per cent of their assessed 'base value', 42 of them had been sold for less than half of this value (Lee and Roselle 2003). Seven firms had a base value of less than zero (liabilities exceeded assets) and had, essentially, to be given away.[8] If these ratios were representative of smaller enterprises throughout China, it would mean that only two-fifths had reasonably healthy to healthy finances in 1999.

The impact of the recession upon non-agricultural workers in the rural areas is hidden from view by a relative paucity of studies, but there is evidence that even before the drive towards reconstruction and privatization that was launched by Jiang Zemin and Zhu Rongji in 1997, they had enjoyed none of the securities enjoyed by urban workers. One study of migration to the urban areas noted that, this had accelerated in the late 1980s because, during the strong, though brief economic contraction in 1989 and 1990, 14.5 million employees had been fired from rural enterprises (Carillo-Garcia 2004). If they had little social security in the 1980s, it is less than likely that they would have had any in the second half of the 1990s.

There was another steep decline in rural non-agricultural employment in the late 1990s. Employment in the TVEs reached a peak of 135.08 million in 1996. In the next 2 years, as the recession took hold of the economy, employment declined by almost 10 to 125.37 million. It did not again reach the level of 1996 till 2003 (CSY 2006: Table 5.4).[9] Even these figures may underestimate the true contraction that took place; for the township administrations suffer from the same inhibitions about firing workers from loss-making enterprises as the central government does about laying off workers from the SOEs. As a result, they kept thousands of TVEs operational on paper but did not pay their workers.[10]

A study of how peasants who lost their land to urbanization were compensated also threw some light, albeit indirectly, on the worsening economic condition of the TVEs. In many of the schemes, families whose land was taken away were given compensation partly in cash and partly in the form of a job in a TVE. But as the TVEs began to lose money, either these jobs did not materialize or the salaries of their workers were withheld. In one city in Sichuan province in 1993, 20,000 people who lost their land were promised jobs but never given them. In a vast number of cases, the salary remained unpaid (Cai 2003b).

9

The Emergence of the Predatory State

Had recession been the only reason for the Chinese workers' and peasants' disenchantment with the reforms, it would not have crystallized into the rising tide of discontent that has so alarmed the leaders of the Chinese Communist Party. But the increased stress that it has put upon these classes and some other identifiable groups like demobilized soldiers, and segments of the intelligentsia (including professors, researchers and journalists), has been turned into active discontent by the simultaneous rise of corruption on a scale many times greater than Chinese leaders had feared when the reforms began.

China took its first steps towards the market in 1978. Yet by the early 1990s, it had already acquired the reputation of being among the most corrupt economies in the world. But does this corruption spell a threat to its stability? Opinion is divided on this because the causal link between corruption and political unrest is not easy to establish. Corruption is a generic term that covers a wide range of rent-seeking activities. Scholars have long argued about this, with some favouring legal and others normative definitions. Most scholars have tended to define corruption as virtually any form of 'improper' behaviour by either a state official or a member of the Communist Party. Ting Gong's definition, for example, includes graft, bribery and misappropriation of public property along with seeking illicit benefits for relatives and friends, neglecting official duties, nepotism and favouritism, shirking, retaliation, making false accusations, filing false reports, boasting and exaggerating, banqueting at public expense, running unauthorized businesses, profiteering, housing irregularities, living lavishly, engaging in improper sexual relations, forming cliques, gambling, whoring, excessive spending on marriages and funerals, engaging in superstitious activities, smuggling, selling state secrets, engaging in insider stock trading, engaging in real estate speculation and fraud, evading taxes, engaging in financial fraud, making illegal and irregular bank loans and diverting and selling disaster relief goods (Gong 1994: 9).

In a landmark book on Corruption and Markets in China, Yan Sun, an associate professor at the city university New York, has used Chinese case books to classify reform-era corruption as follows: embezzlement; misappropriation; bribery; illegal profiteering; squandering; privilege seeking; illegal earnings and smuggling. In addition to these, Chinese law and practice also recognize three other kinds of punishable misconduct—negligence and moral degeneration, and violation of family planning policies. These do not constitute corruption in the normal sense of the term but are frequently cited in Chinese prosecutions. Officials in local government have used these charges extensively to curb popular resistance.

These listings are fairly exhaustive, but not very helpful in assessing the political impact of corruption. All these diverse forms of predatory action become possible only when there is a substantial imbalance of power between the 'contracting parties' and a deliberate abuse of power by the stronger party to enrich himself at the expense of the weaker. But all forms of corruption do not affect the public equally, and are therefore not equally resented by it. The political impact of corruption therefore depends upon not only its prevalence but also its effect. For this purpose, it is more useful to distinguish between three types of corruption. These are embezzlement, that is kickbacks and 'commissions' on purchases and sales (including arbitrage deals based upon insider information), bribery and extortion.

Embezzlement, Kickbacks and Bribery

Kickback, commissions and arbitrage are the most damaging to the economy because they not only divert very large amounts of public funds into private pockets but also bias choices away from the best firms and the best technology towards less satisfactory alternatives. But these are the least obtrusive forms of corruption and therefore have the smallest political impact. The public does end by paying the price in the form of either higher prices or a poorer quality of service, but the impact is spread over virtually the entire population and is very difficult to quantify.

Bribery is more direct, more personal and its cost is easy to quantify. It creates anger or resentment in the bribe giver because it is a reminder of powerlessness. But in the end, this is a transaction from which the bribe giver hopes to gain, so the anger is stifled and does not take a political form.

Both the above forms are essentially private. All parties to such deals have a powerful interest in keeping them secret. The public becomes aware of them only when they see the change in the lifestyle of the corrupt officials over a period of time. But extortion—the third type of corruption mentioned above—is entirely different. For it results directly from an abuse of power by an agent of the state, is 'public' in as much as almost every one who has to deal with the concerned authority has to pay the 'fee'; it affects large numbers of people, whose only gain is the avoidance of harassment. It therefore generates pure, undiluted anger. What is more, since money is extorted to get around various laws, it perverts the purpose and erodes the rule of law. From a protector of the poor the law turns into an enemy of the poor. And since laws are passed by the state, the widespread practice of extortion by agents of the state ends by delegitimizing the state itself in the eyes of the people.

Corruption antedates the period of reform, but in the communist era, the inability to amass wealth limited the types of illegal activities that were possible and the number of ways in which the perpetrator could benefit. These were mainly the falsification of performance reports to please upper echelons of the party and vie for promotions, special postings and privilege; hoarding goods to avoid shortages, and a variety of illicit activities intended to benefit the entire work unit (Kwong 1997). But corruption in its more familiar form appeared the very moment. China took its first steps towards a market economy, for the core ingredient of the change was a willingness to permit the accumulation of income, and therefore wealth, in private hands. As was pointed out in the last chapter, the central leadership allowed this momentous change with considerable reluctance. Indeed had there not been a succession of natural disasters in provinces like Szechuan and Anhui, in the late 1970s, the local cadres might never have mustered the courage to break the mould that the Cultural Revolution had created for agriculture. The second trigger for reform was mounting unemployment. In the urban areas, since the government shouldered the responsibility of finding school and college leavers' jobs, the growing crisis revealed itself in all-pervasive overstaffing and under-employment. There was, however, a limit to how many men the state could employ to do any particular job. Thus, 'confronting higher and higher levels of unemployment, the government had no choice but to free up people and allow them to make a living on their own in privately or township-owned enterprises that operated pretty much outside the state-owned sector' (Qinliang 2000b: Chapter 3). Beginning in 1983, therefore, the government passed a spate of laws that aimed at incrementally achieving three aims: expanding the autonomy of families and enterprises, focusing responsibility for the performance of an enterprise on the plant director and separating ownership from management, giving the enterprises their own legal identity and establishing a modern enterprise system.

But there was a crucially important difference between the unleashing of private incentive in agriculture and in industry. In the former, land was, to all intents and purposes, privatized. So the benefits went directly to the peasants who cultivated it. In industry, however, productive assets continued to be owned by 'the people' and be managed on their behalf by the state. So the cadres whom the reforms 'freed' to operate outside the state sector were not private entrepreneurs—that was to come several years later—but intermediaries acting in the name of the state. This was a situation that begged to be exploited, and once the state ceased to frown upon the accumulation of wealth, the exploitation did not take long to develop. The exploitation was made fatally easy by the demise of the command economy. This gave rise to what Chinese analysts call 'the absolute power of the first in command'.

The first in command is no longer the party secretary, but the head of a local government, state agency or public firm, and his or her unique characteristic is an almost complete lack of accountability to anyone but himself or herself. The rise of the 'first in command' is an inevitable consequence of the state's retreat from centralized planning and its delegation of investment decisions to localities, firms and markets. This began in 1984 when the centre decided to delegate control rights over state-owned enterprises (SOEs) to the local governments. This transferred unprecedented discretionary power to local chief executives while simultaneously removing checks against their misuse.

Except for centrally funded projects, local chief executives have taken over the approving power for critical factors of the economy; at the firm, county, municipal or provincial levels. With hierarchical relations of the Plan system gone, upper administrative echelons are left with few reliable channels to learn about routine violations by lower agencies. From land privatisation to public projects, from financing to public levies, and from SOE reforms to development assistance, local chiefs can sign off approvals at the stroke of a pen. (Sun 2004: 160)

The emergence of a market economy and the resulting commercialization of state power thus created opportunities for self-enrichment that few of the first-in-commands were able to resist.

To cite a few widely known examples from China's prosecutorial records, Governor Cheng Kejie of Guangxi was able to overrule with impunity a provincial decision to allocate a piece of land for the construction of an ethnic theme hall, and give it instead to a mall developer. He also provided him with cheap financing. In another notorious case, the executive deputy mayor of Shenyang, Ma Xiandong, not only approved the allocation of a piece of land to a gang leader, Liu Yong, to build a billion yuan mall in a location where 'every inch was gold', but also waived payment for the land.

The mayor of the same city, Mu Suixin, ran a fraud and embezzlement ring for years, for which he and 120 city officials including Ma Xiandong, were arrested. In an interview he gave after his conviction he revealed few qualms, 'Central decrees and regulations have to be adapted once they reach me. I implement the ones I approve (of), and do not implement the ones I disapprove' (Sun 2004: 161).

Corruption took myriad forms. One of the commonest was to invest the retained surpluses of the enterprise after paying the state's share, in subsidiary enterprises—collectives—that would set up light manufacturing units, shops, service centres, department stores and real estate companies. These would be free of all social obligations to the state and to their workers, and became a favourite avenue for employing the relatives of enterprise directors, factory floor and union leaders and party cadres assigned to the enterprise-level committees. The diversion of post-tax profits from them to new enterprises deprived even the most scrupulously run SOE enterprises of the capacity to modernize, change their product mix and remain competitive in the increasingly competitive market economy that was slowly developing in the country. This virtually guaranteed them a lingering death.

Another was arbitrage: the system of dual pricing—one price for goods supplied under the plan and another for those sold on the free market—which was a part of the gradual shift from a planned to a market economy, created a long interregnum during which money could be made by buying key inputs at the plan prices, supposedly for one's own enterprise, and selling them to users in the non-state sector at market prices. Yet another was asset stripping—selling chunks of factory land, or transferring or selling profitable lines of production in a state enterprise to a newly established subsidiary, collective or private enterprise, which would be owned in all but by the name plant manager, a party chief, a senior administration official, their relatives or all of them together. These sales were in most cases made at throwaway prices, and the parent enterprise, that is the state, was left to shoulder the losses.

Another fertile source of 'primitive accumulation' of capital was speculation in land. Between 1987 and 1992, state authorities at every level from the province to the township acquired land to create special economic zones (SEZs) and development zones, paying only minimal compensation to the peasants who were losing their land with the intention of allotting or selling it to investors and real estate developers. By 1992, no fewer than 6,000 such zones had been established, but more than half never took off (Qinliang 2000b). Many had still not attracted a single investor when they were dissolved by the government of President Hu Jintao in 2005.[1]

But this did not stop local governments from continuing to acquire land. To meet the demands of rapid urbanization, the central government ceded the power to determine land use to the local governments. This opened the way to millions of sweetheart deals between developers and local officials which relentlessly ate into the land available to the peasants. Few of the latter received an adequate compensation.

The government's decision to create a share market, capitalize the large and medium-sized SOEs and allow their shares to be traded in the market, created another opportunity for personal enrichment. In enterprise after enterprise, the managers and party cadres colluded to undervalue the shares, buy or arrange to buy a significant portion and allow the disproportionately high profits and dividends to push up their prices (Qinliang 2000b).[2]

Even bank loans began to command a price. The fact that banking remained almost entirely a state monopoly, and that the funds of state-owned commercial banks were pre-empted by the SOEs, created a premium on advances that bank managers were only too willing to appropriate. In a landmark study by two leading Chinese economists, the director of research at the Peoples' Bank of China, Xie Ping, and his colleague Lu Lei, of the 3,561 bank employees, enterprise managers, farmers and private businessmen whom they interviewed, 82.2 per cent said that bank managers frequently or 'quite often' took bribes to sanction loans. The average bribe amounted to 8.8 per cent of the loans, paid either as an initial bribe or to 'maintain relationships' with the bank afterwards (Pei 2006: 11).

Historically, arbitrage was the first important new avenue for private enrichment opened by the retreat from central planning. In her book, *China: The Pitfalls of Development*, He Qinliang estimates that in 1986 alone the price differential between plan and free market prices created arbitrage opportunities worth 100 billion yuan. Seventy per cent of this, she estimates, ended up in private pockets. The 'earnings' from arbitrage were multiplied by investing in the share market, which was also rife with insider and 'sweetheart' deals, and through speculation in land (Qinliang 2000a: 33). But as the years passed and the market economy matured, the number of avenues multiplied, the amount of money involved in each transaction increased, the corruption rings became more elaborate, reached higher into the party and administration and endured longer before they were exposed and broken up.

Two lists compiled by Yan Sun, of the highest ranking officials arrested and punished for corruption between 1986 and 1990 and 1992 and 2001, reflect the deepening hold of corruption upon the party and the administration, and the growing greed of the concerned officials. In the first period, nine persons holding ranks of deputy minister and above (including provincial governors) were punished. But the bribes they accepted ranged from 5,000 to 38,000 yuan. Most of the bribes were not in cash but were gifts, such as home electronics. Four of the nine did not engage in corruption personally. They were punished for tolerating corruption among their subordinates, business associates and mistresses.

In the second period, there were 13 such cases, but the bribes they took ranged from 64,000 yuan to 40 million yuan ($4.6 million), and 12 out of 13 of them took their bribes in hard cash. In addition, two of them, Chen Xitong, mayor of Beijing for more than a dozen years, and his deputy mayor, Wang Baosheng (who was accused of accepting bribes totalling 25 million yuan but committed suicide before he could be sentenced), built villas for their mistresses out of public money that cost 35.21 million yuan. Finally, while the longest that any of the accused in the first period had remained in office before he was arrested was 8 years. In the second period, it was more than a dozen years—a clear indication that corruption had become more entrenched (Sun 2004: 49–50).

Another unmistakable indication of the way in which corruption is entrenching itself deep within the governmental system is the growing sale of appointments to coveted posts by the senior officials, usually the 'number ones'. In early 2004, the party's committee on discipline issued a circular naming four senior cadres who had sold 168 posts in the late 1990s for just under 3 million yuan. The sale price varied from 13,000 to 49,000 yuan, roughly equivalent to a year's salary (Pei 2006: 145–46). In all these cases, the bribe amounted to roughly a year's salary. Similarly, a list of some of the worst office sellers between 1995 and 2001 compiled by Yan Sun contained 12 more senior party cadres of the level of mayors, party secretaries, governors and their deputies. Six of them received more than 1.2 million yuan for appointing, promoting and transferring 1,015 officials. A seventh overruled his colleagues and took 40,000 yuan to appoint a convicted embezzler to a post in the anti-corruption bureau from where he could monitor and impede the progress of his own case. An eighth, a deputy mayor in Anyang city in Henan province took 139,620 yuan for 18 promotions. One of these was to promote a factory chief, who had earlier been dismissed for misconduct, to the post of deputy mayor (Sun 2004: 50).

The willingness of these officials to raise and 'invest' such a large sum of money in securing a particular post reflects their confidence that they would be able to recoup that amount and much more within a short period of time. What is worse, the willingness of the senior officials to accept these bribes means that they were beneficiaries of, or were prepared to condone, the corruption that was to follow. Corruption had thus ceased to be an individual enterprise and was being carried out by organized networks of cadres in the government departments, in which each participant had his or her cut.

Two examples vividly illustrate the depths to which corruption has poisoned the Chinese State: At the Zhengzhou railway station, three persons, one of whom was the manager of the station's retail service corporation, an official from a provincial utility company and a private business man, were able to secure allocations of space for transporting cargo, outside plan allocations and made millions of yuan by selling it to private and non-state shippers. To persuade the railway officials to look the other way; they gave commissions to no fewer than 50 railway officials (Sun 2004: 56).

On 27 December 2005, a Beijing court convicted Tian Fengshen, who had been the minister for land and resources till 2003, on 17 charges of accepting bribes amounting to 4.4 million yuan ($543,000). Before he became a central minister, Tian Fengshen had been the governor of Heilongjiang province where he had run a well oiled bribery machine from 1995 to 2000. This machine sold positions in government, arranged financing for projects and reclassified farmland so that it could be taken away from the peasants and delivered to real estate developers—for a price. Tian was spared the death sentence because he allegedly confessed and helped the police recover some of the stolen assets, but his position and reputation in Heilongjiang suggest that the half million dollars was only the tip of the iceberg. Tian had been the thinly veiled subject of a best-selling novel about corruption in Heilongjiang, *The Snow Leaves No Trace*.

Tian came under police scrutiny when a fellow member of the Communist Party confessed to it that he had paid Tian 100,000 yuan for arranging a loan and another 800,000 yuan for appointing him the local party secretary. As party secretary, Ma made another 24 million yuan by selling other positions. As the case widened, it decimated the top level of the Heilongjiang administration. Among those fired or jailed were the president of the high court, the top prosecutor, the vice-governor, the deputy head of the legislature and at least 10 mayors and vice-mayors. Ma and another associate, Han Guizhi, were also given suspended death sentences, which were likely to be commuted to life imprisonment (Watts 2005b). But in Harbin, the capital of Heilongjiang, most people believed that many of the members of the corruption ring were still in positions of power. Zhu Shengwen, a former deputy mayor of Harbin, reportedly committed suicide in jail. The official version of his death was that he threw himself out of a prison window, but his family was convinced that he was killed to prevent him from exposing more cases of embezzlement.

One of the most notorious cases of corruption at the highest level was that of Mu Xuichin, the mayor of Shenyang, whose understanding of the powers of 'number one', was described earlier. Mu was given a suspended death sentence in 2001 along with his deputy mayor, Ma Xiangdong. He had been brought to book over his insistence on re-allotting the land intended for an ethnic cultural hall to a known Mafia gang leader to build a mall. He was convicted in 2000 of having accepted more than 6 million yuan (US$1.35 million) in bribes and having more than 2 million yuan in income he could not account for. In an interview he gave to a journalist after his death sentence was suspended, Mu said that he had drifted into corruption unwittingly by accepting a few presents and then growing to like it.

> I thought that receiving bribes meant you had to strike a dirty deal with people in advance. But for my situation, it always happened afterwards—it was always that 'friends' came to see me and gave me money during holidays, when I was sick or at certain occasions. I never knew it was a crime. (*The Straits Times* 2001)

But the truth was a lot uglier. Mu had run a corruption ring in Shenyang. To do this, he had recruited not only his deputy mayor but also at least 120 officials of the Shenyang administration. These included the top prosecutor and the chief judge of Shenyang. Mu was denounced by Zhou Wei, a 70-year-old former Communist Party official. For submitting and organizing petitions to the authorities about the corrupt activities of Shenyang's leaders, Mu sent off Zhou Wei, without trial, to a labour camp in May 1999. His alleged offence was 'disrupting public order'. He regained his freedom only in April 2001 after Mu, Mo and the others had been arrested and sent to jail. But there was considerable evidence that the corruption ring had been much larger, had intimate links with organized crime and that several of its members were still at large. For Mu's arrest did not end the attacks on, and constant harassment of, Zhou Wei. Fearing that other officials who had been part of the corruption ring were still at Beijing, the trials of the 120 officials was moved to other cities (*The Economist* 2001).

In its attempt to curb corruption, the central government has given these and other similar cases wide publicity but they are far from exceptional. According to the Central Commission for Discipline Inspection, nearly 50,000 officials were prosecuted and punished in 2004 and 2005. More than 1,000 cadres committed suicide and 8,000 fled overseas (Watts 2006). While corruption has become more and more entrenched, the central government's capacity to control the behaviour of the cadres in the local governments has continued to slip. According to one study, after the decentralization of the early 1980s, the central government directly monitored only 7,000 officials. Since government and party cadres were the first to benefit from the opportunities that the marketization of the economy created, it is not surprising that the reform era also saw the end of policing by ordinary citizens through denunciation.

The central government has attempted to control corruption among party cadres and in the administration, through three monitoring–cum–prosecution agencies, the Central Discipline Inspection Committee (CDIC) of the CCP, the Ministry of Security of the State Administration (MoS) and the criminal justice system. The CDIC investigated allegations against party members, while the MoS investigated allegations against officials in the administration who were not party members. Those who belonged to both were investigated by both organizations. The CDIC was considerably more important, and more effective than the MoS. The latter was established in 1949, disbanded in 1959 and re-instated in 1986, in a tacit admission that by then a large proportion of the officials in the state administration were no longer party members. It therefore lacked the continuity and experience of the CDIC. Both organizations had a structure that paralleled the structure of the bureaucracy at every level of administration, but in practice, their effectiveness was severely diluted by making the head of the office subordinate to the party committee secretary or the chief administrator at that level. In theory, the local heads of the state security and CDIC offices report both to the local party committee or head of department and to their own superiors at the next higher level. But this provision has been deprived of its teeth by requiring the local disciplinary committee of the CDIC to seek the approval of the party committee, before it can send a case up to the next level of its own organization. There are similar restrictions upon the state security offices (Sun 2004: 168–69).

The most serious drawback of this proviso is that it makes it virtually impossible to prosecute the 'number one', for it requires the CDIC or MoS office to get his permission to prosecute him. The feeling of invulnerability that this provision has given to the chief executives may explain why in Henan province, three heads of the transport department were found indulging in the same malpractices within the short span of 4 years. The exposure and punishment of his predecessors did not deter the successor, because he simply could not believe that he was vulnerable. This was because, throughout this period, the transport chief was also, concurrently, the head of the party branch in Henan (Sun 2004: 170).

There are thousands of similar stories from all over China. The central government's determined, but so far unsuccessful, effort to maintain probity in public life has yielded a rich harvest of data on corruption. They reveal that the number of cases being investigated has grown from 39,000 in 1989 to 174,000 in 2001 (Sun 2004: 47, Table 1.8). Since there are about 11 million persons working in 'public management and social organizations' that is in posts manned by the bureaucracy or party, it means that one in 63 holders of public office or power is prosecuted *every year*. But the same data also reveals how few of the allegations of corruption are actually taken up for formal investigation and how much fewer still are the number of convictions. They also reveal that the reluctance to convict, and if convicted, to punish, rises with the seniority of the accused.

Between January 1993 and June 1997, for instance, the government agencies investigated 731,000 allegations of corruption and penalized 669,000 offenders. The vast bulk of the punishments consisted of fines, demotions and reparations. Only 121,500, or 18.2 per cent were expelled from the party, and only 37,500, 5.6 per cent were convicted on criminal charges (Sun 2004, Table 1.7). By 2004, this figure had dropped to 2.9 per cent (Pei 2006: 152). There is also some evidence of a reluctance to prosecute party members. Pei cites data which show that only one in 10 of the persons prosecuted for corruption in the late 1990s and early 2000s was a party member (Pei 2006: 152).

Extortion

The pervasiveness of corruption—bribery, middleman arbitrage, embezzlement, fraud, the selling of posts and favours and smuggling—has gone some way towards delegitimizing the Chinese political system. Indeed, had it not been for the strenuous, even though only partially successful, efforts of the central government to root out and punish the perpetrators, popular disenchantment would have been far more pronounced. But this disenchantment is by and large passive. It vents itself in cynicism, sarcasm and black humour expressed in doggerel verse and aphorisms. It fuels efforts at reform but not rebellion. To the extent that a threat of rebellion exists, it comes from the rapid spread of another form of predatory behaviour by the party cadres. This is extortion.

In the voluminous literature on corruption, there is little or no reference to its most widespread and politically damaging manifestation—extortion. The lists prepared by Julia Kwong, Tin Gong, Yan Sun, Arthur Wedeman and others neither find explicit reference nor analysis. But this is the most deeply rooted and pervasive form of corruption in China. It is also the most dangerous.

While extortion by officials of the state occurs wherever there are laws that regulate the economic activity of the people, it is most pervasive in the rural areas. One form of extortion, labelled as centralized, or decentralized predation by several authors, a regular feature of the communist era, and indulged by the state itself, was through a systematic under-pricing of agricultural produce. But its origins go further back in time, in the age-old relationship between town and country in China. The second form, however, is new and is peculiarly a product of the capitalist transformation. This is the compulsory acquisition of private land, with inadequate, sometimes virtually non-existent compensation. It is the prevalence of the latter that is the most potent cause of unrest in the countryside today.

Centralized Predation

Forced levies to meet the needs of the state had been a feature of every historical period in China, and had tended to reach crisis levels in the declining years of successive dynasties as other sources of revenue crumbled. The Nanjing government after 1911 and the Guo mindang were no different. The Communists therefore secured the support of the peasantry by declaring that they were committed to simultaneously overthrowing not just the 'three mountains' (imperialism, feudalism and bureaucratic capitalism) but also the 'burden (these had imposed) on the peasants'. After the revolution for the briefest of moments, the peasants did become masters of their own produce. Land reforms between 1949 and 1952 enabled more than four-fifths of the rural population to gain control of the land they cultivated (Jian 2000). But they lost their autonomy once again because of two initially unrelated developments. The first was the reappearance of taxation by local governments to meet their administrative and developmental needs. The second was the pressure that the centre came under, to industrialize and militarize itself during and after the Korean War. To minimize the cost and maximize the efficiency of tax collection, the revolutionary government delegated the task to the local governments. To motivate them and also to enable them to carry out their functions, Beijing allowed them to raise additional taxes on agriculture up to a given proportion of the central levies. But as had happened before and was to happen again, the local governments showed a distressing tendency to become a law unto themselves, even during the heyday of communism. In a report dated 21 October 1952, based upon a survey of 61 townships, Liao Luyang, who looked after agricultural affairs in the party, concluded that the consolidated levies by the local governments on the peasants had already risen to 21.53 per cent of their income (Guidi and Chuntao 2004: 166–95).[3]

Faced with rapidly rising peasant discontent, Mao Zedong issued several stern directives, ordering local governments to bring local-added taxes down to a maximum of 15 and then 7 per cent of the central tax on agriculture. But these had no effect. As a result, he was neither able to reduce the peasants' burden nor able to meet the centre's need for revenue to meet its external challenges. He 'solved' both problems by collectivizing agriculture: in his own words, 'it is hard to take hold of one's hair when it is scattered all over one's head, but easier when it is braided.'

By degrees between 1952 and 1958, 130 million peasant families were gathered into 7 million mutual aid groups, then into 790,000 rural cooperatives and finally into 52,781 communes. By 1958, every last thing that the peasants owned, including their cattle and most household goods, belonged to the commune which became the basic fiscal unit in the countryside. The year 1958 marked the beginning of the Great Leap Forward, which resulted in a catastrophic famine. But barely a decade later, the Great Leap forward was followed by another period of severe disruption during the Cultural Revolution. By 1977, therefore, the living standards of the Chinese peasantry were worse than they had been in the early days of the Peoples' Republic of China (PRC) (Guidi and Chuntao 2004). The peasants expressed their misery through black humour, enshrined in doggerel verse:

A peasant mumbled while digging the ground with a shovel: 'The first three shovelfuls are for turning in grain and taxes to the government; the next three shovelfuls go to the salaries of the commune director, the production brigade leader, and the production team leader; the following three shovelfuls go to those god-damned donations and wasteful banquets eaten by those sons of bitches; and only the tenth shovelful comes to me.' (Guidi and Chuntao 2004: 37)

Decentralized Predation

The introduction of the household responsibility system in agriculture—in effect a return to private farming, in Anhui in 1978 and throughout China by 1980, transformed the peasants' lives. For 6 years, the return to private farming and a substantial increase in grain prices brought bliss to the peasantry, whose income grew by 15 per cent a year. But the new-found affluence of a handful of farmers turned them once again into the natural targets of China's predatory power elite. Even as it made the central government turn its attention back to industry once again, which meant in effect a return to taxation through the under-pricing of farm produce, it attracted the notice, and re-awoke the greed of the local administrations, which too were once again free to levy taxes and determine expenditures within the broad, and necessarily vague, guidelines laid down by the centre.[4] The inevitable happened: In the very next year, 1985, the extra-budgetary revenues collected by the local governments rose to 17 per cent of GDP and amounted to three-quarters of the revenues collected by the central government. Of these off-budget revenues, 55–66 per cent were raised by the local governments (Pei 2006: 142).

The infrastructure for this 'decentralized predation' (that is extortion by local governments and cadres) was created in the very act of dissolving the communes. After the end of the Cultural Revolution, 50,000 plus communes were dissolved and their tasks taken over by some 92,000 townships. In 1984–85, these were brought under 61,766 township administrations. The rationale was exactly the same as Mao had used to collectivize agriculture in the early 1950s. Agriculture was producing surpluses and the surpluses were, once again, to be taxed. To do this efficiently, it decentralized the job and minimized the number of points at which the taxes were collected.

The township administrations were therefore endowed with both fiscal and administrative autonomy. Within a few short years, they had replicated the entire bureaucratic structure of the provincial administration, with six governing branches—the party committee, government, disciplinary committee, people's congress, political consultative committee and armed force department—to oversee all the normal functions of a government: finance, taxation, public security, industry and commerce, transportation, public health, grain administration and agricultural technology, which included water conservancy, seeds, vegetation preservation, agricultural machinery, animal husbandry, food and fishery. Chen Guidi and Wu Chuntao summed it up with a traditional Chinese proverb: 'though a sparrow is small in size, it has everything in its body' (Guidi and Chuntao 2004: Chapter 5).

The township administrations soon developed a life of their own. The number of Communist Party cadres they employed grew from 2.79 million in 1979 to 5.43 million in 1989 and further to 8 million in 1997. The last figure included 1.269 million persons who had been laid off by the SOEs. The average township government had 200–300 employees. Thus, the total numbers employed in rural administration added up to between 20 and 30 million persons (Guidi and Chuntao 2004: Chapter 6).[5] Each administration had to have its complement of cars, office buildings, land lines and mobile phones. Each senior official had to be similarly equipped and all the townships had to cultivate relationships with bankers, entrepreneurs, senior officials and visiting foreign investors through lavish entertainment. These 'administrative expenses' became a huge fixed cost that the township governments had to meet, for no matter who else suffered, the cadres were the last to be laid off or have their perquisites reduced. The peasants summed up their plight as usual in pithy aphorisms: 'How many official hats does it take to crush a straw hat?' and 'Too many dragons will cause a drought' (Guidi and Chuntao 2004).[6]

To cover the growing expenses of local party and government organs and their subordinate agencies, the state added mandatory burdens on agriculture and peasants by way of different 'red documents'. These imposed taxes on agricultural specialties, over and beyond the regular agricultural taxes, regulated the administrative charges and fees to be paid by peasants and labourers, framed guidelines for the creation of village reserves and planned township funds, laid down rules for the use of the accumulated revenue and interest thereon and established the salaries of village cadres. These documents charged the township administrations with building schools in township and villages, implementing family planning, paying various allowances, training the people's militia and constructing roads. All these demands were heaped on the peasants (Guidi and Chuntao 2004: 42). By 1990, according to one estimate made in Anhui province, there were as many as 149 different kinds of levies on the peasants (Guidi and Chuntao 2004: Chapter 6).

The effect of the levies on the peasants was summed up by Lu Xishiu, a veteran party cadre and a pioneer of agricultural reform in Anhui province (where the reforms began in 1978) in a conversation with Chen Guidi and Wu Chuntao, as follows:

> Many of our cadres 'only see buildings without caring who built them; only see straight roadways without caring who paid for them!' No sooner had our peasants improved their lives just a little bit than we started to devour them as if they were the 'meat of Monk Tang.' [In folk literature, Monk Tang's meat was desired because the one who ate it would become immortal!] Anyone can bully the peasants; they are so pitiful. In the past, the household-responsibility system that we started caused a national sensation and had a nationwide impact...(But) What about now? The benefits brought by the household-responsibility system to the peasants have been taken away from them, little by little, by all levels of local government. Today, the situation can be summarized in this way: 'The state quota cannot be fulfilled, not enough can be reserved for the collectives, and nothing is left for the peasants themselves!' 'Who would have thought that our cadres today are so unfamiliar with and so negligent of our peasants, and that there are so few cadres who make friends with the peasants. (Guidi and Chuntao 2004: 27)

Between 1985 and 1991, the central government issued no fewer than four directives to curb the excessive taxation of peasants. These were 'Circular Proscribing Arbitrary Requisition of Donations and Arbitrary Fund-Raising from Peasants', issued in 1985; 'Circular on Effectively Reducing the Burden on the Peasants' issued by the State Council in February 1990; 'Decision on Resolutely Terminating Arbitrary Fund-Raising, Arbitrary Fines and All Kinds of Requisition of Donations' taken by the Central Committee and the State Council in September of the same year and Order No. 92 of the State Council that promulgated the legally binding 'Regulation of Fees Payable by Peasants and Administration of Peasant Labor', released on 17 December 1991. The Li Peng government took the highly unusual step of departing from the normal practice of circulating the order only within the party and the government and making it a public document. It was one of the first efforts by the centre to go over the heads of predatory local governments and somehow empower the peasants but even that did not stop the imposition of fees and illegal levies upon the peasants. In 1991, the per capita net income of peasants nationwide increased by only 9.5 per cent over the previous year in nominal terms, that is at current prices, but the 'fees retained for village reserve and township overall planning' during the same period grew by 16.7 per cent. The year 1991 also saw a change for the worse that relatively few noticed: this was the mandatory substitution of money for voluntary labour. From then on, the fees, taxes, donations and levies had to be paid in cash (Guidi and Chuntao 2004: 18, Chapter 5). Reviewing the causes for the continual rebirth of the same evils Chen Guidi and Wu Chuntao found that

> Each item that was suspended would inevitably affect the interests of some government agency or another and these agencies would soon create a different set of fees that were not included in the list of the explicitly prohibited ones. Even where items were explicitly banned, these agencies would still be able to find new bases for the reinstatement of these same items in a certain document released by the same agency, or in a certain speech drafted by the same agency and given by an official representing the interests of this agency. In some cases, these roundabout routes were not even needed; the documents were simply ignored and no action was taken at all to execute them. (Guidi and Chuntao 2004: 18, Chapter 5)

But worse was still to come. In the end, the central government took the only course open to it. In 1994, it drastically revised the taxation system to snatch back the revenues that the local government had appropriated. While this replenished the central government's depleted coffers, its impact upon local government was little short of disastrous. As was described earlier, within a single year, the centre raised its share of total revenues from 22 to 55 per cent. The share of the local administration therefore fell from 78 to 44 per cent. But there was no corresponding reduction of their administrative and developmental responsibilities. So overnight, the local administrations crashed into debt. According to *China Financial Yearbook*, the total deficit of the counties and townships nationwide amounted to 4.221 billion yuan in 1993 when the tax distribution system was not yet in place. In the year that the tax distribution system was established, the deficit skyrocketed to 72.628 billion yuan, 17 times as high. That figure further increased to 82.77 billion yuan in 1995, continuing its upward trend thereafter (Guidi and Chuntao 2004: 62).[7]

A part of the deficit was made up by the centre through tax transfers to the provincial governments but, as Chen Guidi and Wu Chuntao succinctly noted, the tax reform had transferred rights over revenue upwards and the obligations to spend it downwards. Thus, the provincial governments only passed on to the prefectures what was left after they had met their needs, the prefectures did the same to the counties and the counties did the same to the townships. Since all were strapped for cash, the townships were left to fend for themselves. To enable them to carry out with their responsibilities, the government passed a law that 'allowed' the townships to retain the surplus of the revenue they raised over the sum they had to transfer to the county, and spend it however they wished. The law allowed them to spend the 'surplus collected on their own programmes and assured them that the excess of their expenditures over revenue would be compensated.'

The result was predictable. The county and township administrations not only ratcheted up permitted taxes like the tax on agriculture and that on agricultural special products but also increased their exactions from the peasants and enterprises in their jurisdiction. Chen Guidi and Wu Chuntao reported that according to the statistics of the Ministry of Agriculture, the two agricultural taxes (agricultural tax and tax on agricultural specialties) rose by 19.9 per cent over the previous year in 1995; the 'three retained fees and five overall planned fees' levied on peasants rose 48.3 per cent over the previous year and all kinds of social burdens, including administrative and public institution fees, fines, fund-raising and a requisition of donations rose by 52.22 per cent over the previous year. In the very year, after the so-called tax reforms, the burden on the peasants in one-third of all the provinces, autonomous regions and cities directly under the central government, exceeded the 5 per cent limit stipulated by the state (Guidi and Chuntao 2004).

Data assembled by Minxin Pei support their conclusion for they show that against 55–65 per cent before 1992, 75–95 per cent of the off-budget revenues were collected by local governments after

1994. Eighty-five per cent of these were collected by 'Administrative agencies', mostly in the form of administrative fees and levies (Pei 2006: 142–43.[8]

The tax reform of 1994 was followed within 2 years by the onset of recession in China. As the profits of the TVEs dwindled and more and more of them were forced into loss, the township and village administrations responded by squeezing the peasants even harder. According to Chen Guidi and Wu Chuntao, during 2 years of investigations between 2001 and 2003, they found that local governments exacted as many as 269 items of fees and charges; this tally, they felt, was incomplete because they were not able to get details of several other levies that had been tagged on, but for which it is difficult to find the statistics. Nor were the local governments, the only agencies indulging in this time honoured practice. According to statistics, they gathered from the central government agency that monitors the burden on peasants, at the central level alone, government organs and agencies had issued or created as many as 93 documents or items of charges, fund-raising and requisitions of donation, involving 24 ministries, committees, offices or bureaus (Guidi and Chuntao 2004).[9]

A list of fund-raising activities given by them included a vast range of investments that, in India for example, are routinely funded from tax and non-tax revenues raised by the central and state governments and then devolved to local authorities. These included building village or township offices, schools and theatres; establishing village or township medical clinics, party members' activity centres, propaganda stations for family planning, broadcasting stations and enterprises and fund-raising for improving village or township environments, maintaining a peoples' militia to crack down on crime and so on. Villagers also had to pay various charges relating to education, such as salaries for citizen-financed teachers (who did not receive remuneration from the state directly as other officially recruited teachers did); allowances for state-financed teachers; the cost of building or renovating school buildings; cost of schools' regular administration; fees for newspaper subscriptions and book purchases; and the cost of purchasing teaching equipment and facilities for physical education.

The peasants also paid health fees for the single-child family; allowances for family planning committee members; allowances for family planning task force members and a variety of costs incurred in maintaining a peoples' militia.

The village administration covered other local costs by levying 'administrative fees'. These included village cadres' travel and meals, the renovation of their offices and the expense of village party or Youth League activities and the cost of sending representatives of the party, township or village to village or township people's congresses and the like. Peasants also incur charges in relation to village cadres or personnel released from production. Local 'charges were also levied to pay a variety of income supplements to the branch party secretary, the head of the village committee, the people's militia, the public security committee member, the director in charge of women's affairs, the village team head and the accountants who kept the books. Others on the payroll were the veterinarian, agricultural technician, broadcaster, forest watchman, mountain slope guard, newspaper deliveryman and cleaning staff; the electrician, water technician, carpenter, bricklayer and all other personnel employed in miscellaneous duties (Guidi and Chuntao 2004: 46–7).

Deepening insolvency has not prevented local administrations from undertaking extravagant, demonstrative expenditure. A favourite practice has been to build luxurious buildings to house themselves. These are allegedly always for a social purpose, party offices and administrative, youth, hospitality and entertainment centres. These buildings are not being built only in townships that have become rich or in the more advanced coastal regions but, in keeping up with the Joneses manner, in district centres in poverty-ridden provinces as well. One that drew down Beijing's wrath was a five storey modern building with a manicured garden, built at Zhanjiang in inland Guangdong, that was supposed to be a poverty relief office. The building cost 11 million yuan ($1.45 million) and was built to provide office space to 20 employees. This epidemic of ostentatious official construction made the central leadership issue a warning that if it was left unchecked, it would threaten the Communist Party's hold on power.[10]

Predatory extortion has often become overtly criminal. A striking example was the way in which some party cadres abused the one-child family planning law to extort money from the peasants. Chen Guidi and Wu Chuntao described their experiences as follows:

However, a good policy like family planning can soon degenerate into many terrible local practices once it falls into the hands of village cadres:...A deputy chairman of the People's Congress of Anhui told us that a village in Tanxi county was found during their inspection tours to have fines of more than 3.1 million yuan within just a short month of shock inspections for family-planning purposes. That village was substituting fines for the law. Villagers were allowed to have more births if they paid fines; thus, birth permits became a cash cow. In the 1990s, Tanxi county had as many as 100,000 unregistered children (outside of the family-planning system). The judiciary of Lixin county publicized a particular case that ended in a light sentence for a shocking crime. From December 3, 1998 until May 1999 when the crime was disclosed, three cadres in Sunmiao township of that county, Lin Ming, Yuan Zhidong, and Li Peng, under the pretense of operating a population school, hired ruffians and acquired vehicles. On the false grounds of 'birth beyond planning,' 'unauthorized birth,' 'obstruction of official business,' they took more than 200 innocent villagers away from their homes in the twenty-two villages of Sunmiao township and threw them into private jails. Through the horrendous means of illegal detention, they then extorted large amounts of money from the peasants. Their three private jail rooms were just as scary and dark in the daytime as at night, with all windows sealed and no lighting inside. The stench in the jail rooms was beyond belief as detainees had no washroom facilities. The jailed peasants brought their own blankets and were forced to sleep on the floor in their own filth. It was indeed a ghastly sight... (Guidi and Chuntao 2005: Chapter 5, p. 49)

There was a single motive for imprisoning these peasants–money. Ru Zipei from Shuangmiao village, who had been a migrant worker in other places for many years, had some savings and thus became a major target of extortion. He was taken away on 12 December 1998 and was released 18 days later after making a payment of 8,000 yuan. Three other migrant workers, Zhou Lixun, Zhou Lifu and Zhou Guoyun, were taken away on the same day and detained for 5 days; before they were freed, they had to pay 10,000 yuan. Ma Yuerong, over 60 years of age, from Ruzhai village, had just suffered a house fire and had no money available; as a result, he was jailed for over 170 days. Because of the long detention, he almost lost his hearing capacity. A pregnant woman, named Ma Yin was accused of 'unauthorized pregnancy' and gave birth to a child in the jail; there, she suffered all kinds of torture. When Ma Yin's father, Ma Xueyi and her sister, Ma Sanyin, learned about this and went to the jail to visit her, they were also jailed on the grounds that they would act as prisoner substitutes for Ma Yin.[11]

Chen Guidi and Wu Chuntao had to pay for their courage and their devotion to their country. Presented at the Beijing book fair in 2003, the first print run of 100,000 copies of the full version of their book 'The Life of China's peasants' was sold out within a month. Then, in March 2004, after 150,000 copies had been sold, the authorities took it off the bookstore shelves. The book had been banned by the order of the propaganda department of the Central Committee. Following the ban, an official, Zhang Xide, whom they had named in their investigations, sued them on the grounds that their account of 'The Baimiao township Incident', described in the book was defamatory. Zhang naturally brought up the case in the county of which he had been the party boss, so it was not entirely surprising that he won the case. The local court did not only convict them but also turned the case into a political indictment of the authors. What is more, the national media, which had hailed the book suddenly went silent and did not cover the farcical proceedings of the court. The court proceedings ended in October 2004 but it gave no verdict for more than a year. During this period, in December 2004, a newly appointed party secretary for Anhui province denounced the book and a party newspaper, which had been serializing the authors' next book on an uncorrupt judge, abruptly stopped doing so. On the same day, a gang of hooligans pelted their two room apartment with bricks. No one came to investigate. Shortly after that, Chen Guidi was asked to resign from his job. The stone throwing continued night after night for 20 nights till the couple and their child fled from Hefei, the capital of Anhui, where they lived and hid in a remote corner of the poor, south-eastern province of Jiangxi (Guidi and Chuntao 2006).

Chen Guidi and his wife may have been persecuted but their work did not go unnoticed. The 2004 bluebook of Chinese Society, published by the Chinese Academy of Social Sciences, confirmed the rise of tension in the rural areas and the close connection this had to the recessionary conditions that developed in the late 1990s (Fewsmith 2004). 'One of the chief sources of social tension', it concluded, 'is the tendency of the politically well connected in the rural areas to take care of themselves and ignore the needs—or worse, actively harm the interests—of the remaining population'.

In a significant admission, the bluebook confirmed that the predatory relationship between cadres and peasants developed out of the freedom that the township administrations were given to manage their own budgets. In the years of plenty, between 1980 and 1995 they hired staff with abandon, only to have their revenues dry up, first because of the 1994 tax reforms and then because of the failure in the 1990s of a large proportion of the TVEs. The drying up of other sources of revenue had forced the majority of them into debt. Approximately one-third of the counties and two-thirds of townships were in debt. As a result, 80 per cent of townships were facing difficulties in paying wages regularly. The bluebook confirmed the findings of independent researchers (cited in Chapter 3) that this forced the townships into debt and into extorting more and more money from the peasants. According to Zhao Shukai, a researcher at the State Council's Development Research Center, in 2004 the number of cadres at the township level was about three times what it had been in the 1980s. County and township governments therefore accounted for 20 per cent of total fiscal revenues but supported 71 per cent of public employees.

The bluebook also conceded that the rising rural tension was a product of the conflict between cadres at every level of the local administration and the peasantry. Agriculture continued to suffer from hidden taxation, through delays in the adjustment of output prices by the state. In spite of this, higher levels in the administrative hierarchy continued to demand that revenues be sent up. The townships did not have the strength to resist, so they in turn increased their demands upon the peasantry. In 2004, township finance had reached an impasse: the township cadres had little idea how to solve their debt problems and as a result, faced pressures from above and resistance from below (Fewsmith 2004).

As did the laid-off industrial workers, the peasants expressed their powerlessness by composing doggerel verse:

> Seven hands, eight hands, everybody extends hands to the peasants.
> You collect, I collect, he collects, and peasants are distraught;
> You solicit, I solicit, he solicits, and peasants are upset.
> Demand grain, demand money, and demand life;
> guard against fire, guard against theft, and guard against cadres.
> (Guidi and Chuntao 2005: 21)

Migrant Labour

The other main sufferers from the onset of recession and the increase in predatory behaviour by the cadres are the migrant workers. The migration of labour from rural areas to the cities and new centres of industry has been a key ingredient of China's shift from a centrally planned to a market economy because it has created the flexible labour market, a necessary pre-condition for the hectic industrialization of the SEZs and the cities and townships. But the development has come at a substantial cost to the migrants. Data gleaned from surveys of 5,516 migrant households, conducted in 12 cities in 2001 and 2005, showed that although migrant labour households earned similar amounts in terms of money incomes as resident families, they did so only by working far, far harder. In five very large cities included in the survey, the migrants earned an average of 4.6 yuan an hour, while the residents earned 14.7 yuan. In all the 12 cities, nearly all adults in migrant families worked and they worked on an average 64 hours a week. By contrast, very few resident families had more than one working adult member and he or she worked on an average for just over 40 hours a week. Only by working so hard could migrant families overcome the difference in wage rates (Park and Wang 2006).

The cause is the Household Registration or Hukou system which, through most of the days of the Communist State, linked the civic rights enjoyed by the citizen to his place of residence. The Hukou system is as old as China itself, for its roots can be traced back to the Xia dynasty, which ruled from the 21st to the 16th century BC. Often modified but never annulled, it has remained a prime tool of governance in the Chinese state ever since. But in pre-communist China, it was used by successive dynasties for taxation, conscription and the gathering of vital statistics only. Although a sharp urban–rural divide was a constant feature under all dynasties, the Hukou system did not deny the Chinese, the freedom to move to and settle in any part of the country. This freedom was expressly reiterated by the PRC in 1949 and again in 1954 but its decision to concentrate on industrialization, which was of necessity urban centred, led to what came to be called a 'blind flow' of migrants from the villages into the towns (Lijiang 2003). To check this, the PRC enacted a Regulation of Household Registration enactment in 1958. Thenceforth, citizens enjoyed access to all public utilities and services, only in their place of residence. This included employment, food coupons, housing, education for children, health and old age benefits.

Indeed, the very first step towards the transformation of the Hukou system was taken in 1955, when the central government introduced food rationing in the country. The Hukou system therefore chained the rural population to the villages and since, under the thrust for industrialization, most of the jobs in the modern sector being created were in the cities, over time it created a new kind of urban–rural divide that Chinese scholars increasingly compare to the caste system in India. The resemblance to the Indian caste system was reinforced by the fact that no matter where a child was born, he or she was given the Hukou of the mother's original place of residence. This condemned the rural population to relative poverty, but since there was little scope for migration, this did not create an awareness of the glaring disparity between urban and rural living standards that was to develop later.

The opportunity to migrate to the cities reappeared only after the restoration of private farming through the household responsibility system in 1978–80 created large agricultural surpluses that the peasants were able to sell in the urban markets. This created a free market for food and loosened the iron grip of food rationing upon the freedom to move within China. Like most sections of society, migrant workers initially gained hugely from economic liberalization. By 1995, there were around 80 million such workers who spent more than 200 days a year in urban areas.[12] From their earnings, they were sending $35 billion a year back to their families in the villages from where they had come. Not only were they, themselves, earning up to seven times as much in industry as they had done in agriculture but by moving out of the villages they also reduced the workforce that was dependent on agriculture and raised its average productivity by approximately one-third (World Bank 1997: 45).[13]

But by the early 1990s, the flood of rural migrants had awakened fears of a 'blind wave' of farmers entering the cities and created a backlash among the urban residents. This caused the city authorities to harden the Hukou system in a variety of ways. Migrants had to furnish a variety of permits before they could secure work or be given a temporary residence permit. These were an identity card from the parent county, a temporary residence certificate from the police for the city where he or she works, to be renewed each year, an employment certificate from the home county and an employment card from the labour bureau of the city in which he or she was working. These were introduced by the Ministry of Public Security, ostensibly to keep a check on migration, but as with all similar laws they became excellent pretexts for extortion by local authorities.

Not surprisingly, therefore, migrants had to pay for each of these permits, not only the stipulated fee but also a much larger 'consideration' to the cadres, manning the government bureaux. A sample survey by the Ministry of Labour, in 1996 showed that against stipulated fees totalling 20 yuan, migrants were paying 223 yuan to get their cards. These levies cut into their already meagre earnings and forced them to work longer hours to earn the minimum they needed to sustain themselves and their families back in the villages (Zhao 2001).

Migrants were discriminated against in another subtle way: for example, in 1995, the Beijing municipal government enacted regulations aimed at tightening the control of housing rental to rural migrants. The regulation stipulated that any institution or person, leasing house to non-Beijing residents, must obtain a house-leasing certificate from the district or county government and renew the certificate annually. The house or apartment must be privately owned in order to be eligible for renting and must be certified by police bureau for meeting safety standards. The owner must sign affidavits with police bureaus and family planning agencies, agreeing to be responsible for preventing crime and over-quota births in the house or apartment. He also had to pay a fee equivalent to 2 per cent of the annual rent. This regulation had the predictable result of making housing both less available and more expensive for the migrants (Zhao 2001).

Unlike urban residents, who are primarily employed in manufacturing and other industries, rural migrants are concentrated in service and construction industries. Most migrant workers take up physically demanding jobs as manual labourers, textile and garment factory workers, toy factory workers and service workers. Indeed, they mainly occupy jobs that local residents disdain.

The greatest difficulty migrant parents face is that the educational expenses are too high. This stops them from sending children to the public schools. Indeed, the opportunity for education is also closely tied in with the Hukou system. Children who are registered residents in the cities are entitled to 9 years of schooling. One study found that migrant families have to pay an annual fee ranging from 3,000 to 30,000 yuan per child to have their children enter public schools (Fleisher and Yang 2003). Every problem that the migrants face was encapsulated by the *New York Times* on 3 April 2006 when, in a report on migrant scavengers at the Shanghai municipal dump. The job was as dangerous as, to pull out plastic, shoe soles, unbroken bottles and the like, all of which fetched good money in the market, the scavengers had to compete with an Australian company which was using heavy machinery to dump the garbage in a modern landfill. Several scavengers had met their deaths, crushed by this machinery. But so desperate was the hunt for a livelihood that this was not the only threat the scavengers faced. An equally potent threat was of being preyed upon and robbed by rival gangs of scavengers. Yet there was no dearth of scavengers, because the earnings were good. Son Liping, one of those whom the newspaper interviewed, said that he preferred this work because it was the only way in which he could afford to pay the 10,000 yuan ($1,250) registration fee to send one of his daughters to a local high school and to pay 1,000 yuan ($125) a month for the education of a second daughter in a primary school (French 2006).

A 2003 survey of 4,714 rural migrants in Shanghai revealed that only 14 per cent had health insurance and 10 per cent had pension plans, whereas 79 and 91 per cent of local employees had health insurance and pension plans, respectively. Although it is compulsory for employers in urban cities in China to contribute to unemployment funds set up by the government, these funds are available only to local residents. Migrant workers who work in the same units were not entitled to unemployment benefits (Wong et al. 2007).

From 1996 onwards, as recession tightened its grip on the Chinese economy, the insecurity of the migrant labourers began to increase. According to urban price and living standards data, in 1996, 37.5 per cent of urban households reported a drop in living standards. The decline was unevenly distributed, for while 54 per cent of those in the lowest quintile experienced a fall, only 3.8 per cent of those in the highest quintile did so. In 1997, the proportion of losers in the lowest quintile increased to 60 per cent and in the highest to 20 percent (Cook 2002). Since migrant workers fell squarely into the lowest quintile, they were the main victims of recession. These were, however, the early days of recession. It is therefore safe to assume that the condition of the migrant workforce did not improve during the rest of the decade.

The growing pressure of unemployment also hardened the attitude of the urban residents towards the migrants. This has led to a heightened feeling of insecurity and has legitimized their persecution by minions of the state. The growing feeling of insecurity has told on the mental health of migrants. This is clearly reflected in the very few studies of the mental health of migrant labour that have been undertaken so far. Data from one very small-scale study in 2002 suggested that migrant workers experience a high level of anxiety and feel nervous, upset and unhappy. Another study by X.F. Li, in 2004, showed that 60 per cent of the 106 migrant workers, interviewed, experienced mental health symptoms related to anxiety, depression, hostility and interpersonal sensitivity. A detailed study of the mental health of 83 migrants, using six indicators of mental health also concluded that 63 per cent of migrant workers were suffering from, or prone to, developing mental health problems (Cook 2002).

From the viewpoint of political stability, what is more disturbing is that the growing hostility of the urban residents has legitimized predatory behaviour by the petty bureaucracy and the police. Apart from the ubiquitous need to pay bribes, the police and other functionaries have preyed upon migrants regularly. The usual method is to demand that migrants produce their various permits and certificates, insist that they are not in order and demand a bribe to overlook theirs. As with their rural counterparts, if the migrant workers resist, they are taken to the police stations and beaten up or imprisoned, till they see sense.

In the end, no amount of data can capture the living conditions of the migrant workers as well as their own stories. The first story below is of Suiling. Far from being a victim, Suiling ranks among the beneficiaries from migration, for she has a family and between herself and her husband makes a reasonable living:

> She is only 36 years old. Yet when you look at her, you know that every part of her is wearing out. Her whole body sags. Sometimes she works all day and through the night into the early hours of the morning. After all, there are many costs that come with living in the city. And she has many people in her family to support. Li Siuling is a migrant worker: just one of 130 million who have left their rural communities to find work in the prosperous eastern cities. The money that she and others like her send back now makes up more than half of the income of the peasants and rural workers in the Chinese hinterland.

Suiling was only 15 when she left Anhui province, not far from Shanghai. It was soon after her father had died. On offer in the city were the menial, dangerous or difficult jobs that are always poorly paid. At first she worked in a restaurant, making 100 yuan a month, while the city citizens working with her earned five times that amount. Then she sold clothes, earning 350 yuan, while her urban colleagues took home 900. It was just one of the prejudices that she has had to face.

There are four others. After 20 years—like most Chinese citizens who move away from the household where they are officially registered—she still pays an annual fee for a temporary residence permit. Effectively, it registers her as a second-class citizen within her own country. It deprives her of a vote in the local elections. It deprives her children of the right to free education. It exposes her to harassment from a police force, strapped for cash. Indeed, the police came to her house around midnight once, demanding to see her permit. When she produced it, they tore it up in front of her. Then they fined her for not being able to produce her documents and jailed her when she would not pay.

The fifth prejudice cursing migrant workers has largely escaped her. Many who have lived in the city for as long as she has done are often unmarried and socially dislocated. But she has a husband—a migrant worker like her from her province. (Richards 2004)

The second story is of Sun Zhigang, a college-educated fashion designer from Hubei, the capital of Anhui province, whose wrongful arrest, detention and custodial death in Guangzhou in April 2003 led to a national outcry that compelled a change of regulations governing the treatment of migrant workers by the Guangzhou administration. A Human Rights Watch report summarized the newspaper's findings as follows:

On 25 April 2003, a daily newspaper in Guangzhou which is renowned for its investigative journalism published the following report:

'Sun was stopped on his way to an internet cafe by local police who asked him to show his identity card and temporary living permit. The temporary living permit (or *zanzhuzheng*) was a document then required for visiting workers from other provinces. Sun had forgotten to bring his identity card with him, and had not yet obtained a permit. As was then common practice, Guangzhou police took Sun to the local police station. Sun called his roommate, Cheng, from the police station on a mobile phone and asked Cheng to bring money for bail and Sun's identity card. Cheng did so, but was told by police that Sun could not be released on bail—most likely, Cheng learned, because "Sun had 'talked back' during his interrogation.

The following day, Sun was transferred to a migrant detention center. Again, he called friends and asked for help. Sun's supervisor went to the detention center to attempt to get Sun released on bail. However, he "was told to come back the following day, because staff were about to go off duty." Later that day, Sun's friends called the detention center again and learned that Sun had been transferred to the medical clinic within the detention center. Again, Sun's roommate Cheng tried to visit Sun in the clinic, but was turned away by staff who said that only family members could visit. On March 20th, Sun's friends called the clinic and learned that Sun had died of, reportedly, a heart attack. According to the article, "Sun's previous medical history had shown no sign of heart problems."

Sun's family and friends requested an autopsy of his body at Zhongshan University. The autopsy center of Guangzhou's Zhongshan University delivered a report on April 18th, indicating that Sun had died in shock and that he had been heavily beaten on the back and many other places on the body. Evidence of heavy hemorrhaging was found in the back and the muscles on his sides. A doctor who wished to remain anonymous told the reporter that Sun must have been beaten several times, for the hemorrhage was very unusual and serious.

Doctors from Zhongshan University were all stunned by the brutality. One of the doctors said that Sun was not only beaten on the back and buttocks, but that his knees were also burned. All the facts clearly showed that Sun was beaten to death.

Reporters from *Southern Metropolitan Daily* who requested an interview with the relevant police station were refused. The article notes, "Before Sun left the detention centre for the clinic, the police asked him to sign his name on a document. Sun wrote, 'Satisfied! Thank you! Thank you!'

Sun's father, who lives in a rural area of Hubei province, expressed regret to *Southern Metropolitan Daily* reporters that he had gone to great lengths to get a university education for his son. "If he hadn't gone to university, he wouldn't have been so bookish as to argue about his rights, and he wouldn't have been killed," he said'. (Human Rights Watch 2007)

It is reasonably certain that Sun Zhigang was being shaken down for a bribe by the police and died because he refused to pay. The public outcry unleashed by the story made the central government and the Guangzhou administration take rapid action. On 10 June 2003, the Guangzhou municipal intermediate court sentenced 12 persons to sentences ranging from 3-years imprisonment to death. One person, the principal assailant in the hospital, was sentenced to death and an accomplice given a death sentence with 2-year reprieve; two others received life sentences and the remainder between 3 and 15 years in prison. Six other officials were sentenced to 2-years imprisonment for their complicity.

Sun's case triggered a major debate on the validity of the holding system and the two-decade-old Measures for Internment and Deportation of Urban Vagrants and Beggars, which were issued by the State Council in 1982 and were the legal basis for internment and deportation by public security authorities. By 2003, the powers it gave to the police and other city authorities had become widely used instruments for extortion from the poor. Sun resisted because he was well-educated and already had a job. But had he not been so, and had he not had a group of friends and employers who valued him, his case would never have been investigated, let alone hit the headlines. The central government understood this and used the occasion to abolish the law permitting deportation altogether (*China Daily* 2003).

Land Grab—the Final Straw

The control that peasants regained over the use of their land in 1978–80 proved short lived. In 1986, the central government passed a Land Management law which allowed local village authorities to lease land to entrepreneurs, in exchange for compensation. Following its policy of 'Fording the River by Feeling the Stones', the central government allowed Shenzhen to begin the experiment first, in 1987. Shenzen's successful auction of several pieces of land led in 1989 to a decree of the National Peoples' Congress, allowing land to be leased to non-village and non-agricultural users. In May 1990, the State Council followed this up by promulgating decree no. 55 entitled

'Temporary rules governing the sale and lease of land in Municipalities and townships' of the Peoples' Republic of China'.

The purpose of these laws was to create the beginning of a land market that would meet the growing need for non-agricultural land. But the competition to corner productive resources that economic reform and fiscal decentralization unleashed, turned it rapidly into a new and potent threat to the peasantry. As in the case of industry, the root cause was the local cadres' reluctance to surrender all the powers that they enjoyed before. When, in a bid to end chronic food shortages, various local governments decided to restore the right to decide what to produce to the farmers and to allow them to reap the benefits, instead of transferring ownership of land to him and his family, they transferred only the right to cultivate the land. Ownership remained with one or other form of rural collective. Thus a nationwide investigation of 271 villages suggested that even in the late 1990s, rural land ownership belonged to different rural collectives. Among these villages, 105 regarded the administrative villages as land owners and 119 held the small production groups as owners. In 39 villages, the land was owned by both the village and the small group. In no village did an individual peasant own any land. As a result when it became possible to sell land to industrialists and real estate developers, the decision rested in the hands of the cadres that controlled the village administration. What is more, since larger projects would require the surrender of land spread across several villages or small team holdings, the township or county cadres would also get into the act of selling the land (Cai 2002a).

Since there was no real land market, peasants found it difficult to estimate the value of the land that was being taken away from them. Being powerless, they got only what the cadres at the upper levels of local government deemed it necessary to pay them. The compensation was therefore not only small but also totally arbitrary. In the suburban areas at the fringes of the cities and larger towns, it was customary to give peasants a regular salaried job as part of the compensation. But as was reported earlier, in one city in Sichuan province, for example, by 1993 more than 20,000 peasants had failed to be allocated jobs after their land was taken away. In some villages in the suburbs of Shanghai, many peasants were not allocated jobs because there were not enough positions. Consequently, they received a 200 yuan subsidy each month which was less than their income from farming (Cai 2002a: 664–666).

Things were no better when the compensation was entirely in cash. As investment from Hong Kong flowed into the Zhou Hai, Shantou, Guang Zhou and Pearl river delta areas, it sparked an instant frenzy to open up SEZs. Townships and municipalities in these provinces put vast tracts of land on the leasehold market. So great was the frenzy that in 1992 an estimated tenth of the entire capital raised in the Hong Kong market was sucked into these provinces. Their success caused the rest of the country to jump on the band wagon. Between the end of 1992 and mid-1993, the entire country joined in the race to open SEZs. Money poured in also from Taiwan and South Korea. In 1993, by some estimates, nine-tenths of the fresh capital flows into China went into the real estate market (Qinliang 2000b).

It was the old story once again. No sooner had the central government created the tiniest crevice through which the local governments could make money, than the latter had rushed in pell-mell. Data published by Beijing's Ministry of Construction and quoted by He Qinliang, showed that by March 1993, no fewer than 6,000 SEZs had been opened. These had swallowed 15,000 sq.km (1.5 million hectares) of land. That was 1600 sq.km more than the total urban area of China. This estimate did not include huge swathes of land that the township and village administrations had appropriated to create so-called 'Development Zones'. There was a near-complete loss of control by Beijing over the provinces and by the latter over the townships and villages. The supply of land for SEZs and DZs so far exceeded demand that much of the land remained unutilized, and remains so till this day. Not surprisingly it was the less attractive central provinces that suffered the most. Hunam province, for example, enclosed 2,485 sq.km of land in more than 300 SEZs. The wire fencing went up, and the billboards advertising a glorious future adorned all the approaches to them. But the province never found the resources to invest in the infrastructure. As a result, the billboards were all the development that took place (Qinliang 2002b: 61).

What these SEZs did irrevocably was to destroy farmland. The Ministry of Agriculture estimated that by the end of 1992, the SEZs had swallowed 10 million *mu* or 667,000 hectares of farmland. A cadastral survey of the province of Guangdong in 1996 showed that local authorities had sequestered 1.3 million *mu* of farmland for large-scale projects. This was half of all the arable land in the province.[14] Cai also noted that by 1996, the amount of land acquired in the 'zone frenzy' but left undeveloped totalled 1.74 million *mu*, of which 53 per cent was originally farmland. Half the idle farmland could no longer be converted back for farming purposes. In the process of this large-scale land conversion, many local governments occupied farmland at will and did not pay enough attention to the compensation for peasants.[15]

When local governments are approaching insolvency, but are in the grip of a land enclosure frenzy, someone has to suffer. Needless to say it was the peasants. Drawing upon a large number of surveys, Yongshun Cai notes that county and prefectural governments would keep 30 per cent or more of the lease proceeds to meet 'expenses of sale'. In some places, it was as high as 70 per cent. In the nation as a whole, between 1987 and 1994 'fees' collected from the leasing of land totalled 242 billion yuan, with most which the local governments kept in their extra-budgetary accounts. It was estimated that about 60–70 per cent of the profits from land conversion went to the government or its agencies and about 25–30 per cent was collected by the village government, whereas peasants received about 10 per cent (Cai 2002a: 671).

The threat that such a rapacious land grab posed to the livelihoods of the farmers is illustrated by one example that Yongshun Cai gives:

> One such example is the lease of land in a village in Guangdong province. This village had 140 households and more than 760 people in the early 1990s. In 1993, the town government decided to lease 7,000 *mu* of land to a businessman from Hong Kong to build villas and a golf course. 'The village in question was asked to turn in 577 *mu* of land. This deal dramatically reduced the portion of paddy farmland per capita in the village from 1.4 *mu* to 0.18 *mu*. When converting land, the major village leaders held an extended Party-member meeting and announced the plan of the township government, declaring that it had to be accepted unconditionally. At this meeting, many had voiced their objections, but their opinions were ignored. All decisions were made by the upper-level government and the then village head. The town government not only made the decision for the village but also controlled the money collected from the lease. According to the agreement between the town government and the Hong Kong businessman, the lump-sum compensation for one *mu* of land was 10,000 *yuan*. But the actual amount paid to the town was 8,000 *yuan* with the other 20 per cent being retained by parties other than the village' (The money, however, did not come to the peasants). Since most of the land had been converted, the town government planned to use

the 4.61-million-*yuan* compensation to build factory buildings for lease which would be the major source of income for the villagers. The problem was that the town government did not allocate the money to the village all at once; instead, it was distributed piecemeal, hundreds of thousand of *yuan* each time. Due to the shortage of money for building materials and the salary of workers, the construction of the factory houses lasted five years and still had not been completed at the time this event was reported. But by then the funds for compensation were depleted. The loss of land and the failure of the project as a new source of income posed a severe problem for peasants in the village. (Cai 2002a: 672)

There could have been several reasons for this decision to convert what should have been a capital sum into an annual income stream. But all of them would originate in the insolvency of the townships and that in turn can be traced back to the slackening of economic activity that began towards the end of 1994. After the loss of land, the peasants repeatedly presented their grievances and demands to higher level governments, but none of their complaints were heeded. When they visited the township administrations, their complaints were 'alluded to' but left unaddressed. It was hardly surprising that the already antagonistic relationship between peasants and cadres was intensified.

The above case, in a village that Yongshun Cai refers to simply as 'N', is the rule rather than the exception. The simultaneous absence of a land market, from which peasants can get a valuation of the land they are losing and anything approaching ownership rights, makes it almost impossible for them to resist summary eviction with little or no compensation. In provinces where industry has mushroomed, the peasants are at least able to fall back on non-agricultural employment to safeguard their incomes and millions have emerged as net gainers from the change. But even in these provinces, as the pattern of rural unrest shows, the dispossession has rankled. In Guangdong province, where half of the arable land was seized to set up SEZs, before 1992 petitions by peasants concerning land conversion accounted for half the total number of petitions (Tiejun and Shouyin 1996).[16] But the subsequent attempts at checking the frenzy did not stop the blind rush for land. In 1998, the Central State Council Letters and Visits Office received 460,000 letters and appeals from the whole country, of which issues concerning peasants accounted for two-thirds. Unauthorized fee collection, usurpation of farmland and corruption were the most common complaints (Cai 2002a). Some lower level cadres admitted that peasant burdens and loss of farmland have been the two most serious issues that threaten stability in rural China (Cai 2002a).

But the rising tide of protest has not stemmed the inexorable expropriation of land from the peasants. In a shocking admission in 2006, the director of law enforcement in the Land Ministry, Zhang Xinbao, said there have been more than a million cases of illegal land use in the past 6 years (Watts 2006). A National Land Use Survey conducted by the Ministry of Land and Resources in October 2006 and released in April 2007 showed that China had lost another 3,082 sq.km of arable land in the first 9 months of 2006 to non-agricultural uses. To the Ministry's knowledge, 603 sq.km of this—more than 60,000 hectares—had been illegally acquired by local governments for non-agricultural purposes in 131,000 separate cases. That was 131,000 more defrauded peasants. The latest loss had brought down the arable acreage to 1.226 million sq.km. This was only 20,000 sq.km above the danger level of 1.206 million sq.km which the Ministry considered the minimum that China needed to feed itself (Huifeng 2007).

10

Retaining the Mandate of Heaven

The manner in which recession (or 'slowdown') and the rise of a predatory state apparatus came together to sharpen social conflict and erode the authority of the state, did not go unnoticed within the government and the Communist Party. In January 2006, the media reported that the number of 'disturbances against public order' had risen from 74,000 in 2004 to 87,000 in 2005. This was 10 times the number of 'incidents' in 1993.[1] Official publications, like the Blue Book on Chinese Society, published by the Chinese Academy of Social Sciences (CASS), referred more and more frequently, and freely, to the threat that rising discontent poses to social stability.

In a country as vast as China, even 87,000 incidents does not sound like a great many. The Chinese government's own account of unrest, for one, is extremely broad and non-specific. In the aforementioned release of 2005 figures on social unrest, the Ministry of Public Security (MPS) labelled them as 'disturbances against public order'. A ministry spokesman later clarified that the 87,000 number did not solely refer to mass protests but also to all criminal cases linked to public disorder, such as 'mob gatherings, obstruction of justice, fighting and trouble-making' (Monteleone 2006). Both the definition and the clarification show that only disputes that could not be settled fairly amicably by the local authorities were included in the list. These were only a small fraction of the overall corpus of discontent in Chinese society. A parallel set of data presented by Elizabeth Perry suggests that the listed disturbances formed only a tiny proportion of the actual number of disputes between the people and the authorities. Citing China's Foreign Broadcast Information service, she pointed out that in 1993, the countryside witnessed some 1.7 million cases of resistance, primarily tax resistance, of which 6,230 cases were classi-fied as 'disturbances' (*naoshi*) that entailed severe damage to persons or property. The confrontations that year exacted a staggering toll of deaths and injuries on some 8,200 township and county officials (Perry 2001). In sum, all the 8,700 disturbances in 1993 and the 87,000 in 2005 were challenges to the authority of the state, although of varying degrees of seriousness.

The decision to highlight the rise of discontent was the beginning of a profound reorientation of policies in Beijing. This was spear-headed by President Hu Jintao and Prime Minister Wen Jiabao and reflected their growing anxiety over the gradual erosion of the party's authority in the country. This touched a nerve that ran far deeper in the Chinese consciousness than the communism that Mao Zedong had implanted. The fear of rebellion against a ruler who was perceived to be unjust had been a leitmotif of Chinese thought, through the ages.[2] This did not change with the formation of the People's Republic of China (PRC) in 1949. It underscored the ambi-valence towards the market economy—attraction to its efficiency and repulsion towards its inherent inequity—characterized by the policies of *Fang* (letting go) and *Shou* (tightening up) (Baum 1994: 5–9), between 1978 and 1989. The relaxation of price and production controls, and decentralization of investment decisions in the early 1980s led to a huge spurt in economic growth but also triggered rapid inflation which impoverished students, professionals and workers and corruption, which rewarded unscrupulous elements within the party. The resulting unrest culminated in the showdown at Tiananmen.

Tian Anmen forced a choice upon the reformers. After much re-flection, Deng Xiaoping concluded that the party had no choice but to push ahead with growth, as fast as possible and hope that the gainers would sufficiently outnumber the losers, to enḋure political stability.

Deng Xiaoping unveiled his choice during his southern tour of 1992. It was turned into formal policy by President Jiang Zemin and Premier Zhu Rongji in 1998. However, their timing could not have been worse, for their thrust towards structural reform and their reliance on the trickle down effect of growth—to resolve social contradictions—coincided with the onset of a recession that lasted till the end of the decade. Most of the workers that they laid off in millions did not therefore find new jobs, or had to make do with less well-paid and more insecure work.[3]

But the sharp rise in social unrest did not dampen Jiang Zemin's commitment to growth and modernization. In a landmark speech in July 2001, at the 80th anniversary of the founding of the CPC, he sketched out his ideas on the challenges that the Communist Party would face in the coming years. Jiang Zemin developed his thesis in impeccably Marxist terms. Recalling the relationship between the economic base and the social and political superstructure of society, he warned that if the CPC did not adjust constantly to the changes in the former, it would become an 'obstacle to the development of the productive forces and social progress'. Jiang urged the party to recognize the economic and social differentiation that had set in as a result of economic reforms, and urged the party to change its structure accordingly. To make sure that the party remained the standard bearer of this 'advanced culture', Jiang proposed that membership be thrown open to China's new technocrats, managers and outstanding entrepreneurs from the private sector.

As was shown in Chapter 3, when Chinese data are cleansed of their political bias, it can be seen that Jiang's all-out thrust towards growth was not a conspicuous success, because it coincided with the onset of recession in 1997. What it did was to discourage the leadership from taking any notice of the problems that the neglect of equity in the face of mounting recession was creating. The leadership's adamant refusal to acknowledge that there had indeed been at least a sharp 'slowdown' and not a 'soft landing' after the investment spree of 1991–95, made it all the more difficult for the sceptics to make themselves heard. As a result, the regime largely ignored the mounting number of 'mass incidents' taking place all over China. These began to receive sustained attention only after Hu became the general secretary of the party and the nation's president. But even the new administration did not publicize the rapid escalation of unrest in the urban working class. The number of labour disputes increased from 1,909 in 1994 to 22,600 in 2003. The number of workers involved increased from 77,704 in 1994 to 800,000 in 2003. This was a 10-fold increase within a decade.[4]

The worst sufferers were laid-off workers, migrant workers and peasants. CASS released data which showed that by 2004 migrant workers made up half of the entire urban workforce.[5] Although many of them had already been living and working in urban areas for years, they were still treated as second-class citizens, denied permanent residency permits, insurance and social welfare benefits, and were perennially open to extortion by the police and petty officials.

Crisis of Legitimacy

In July 2001, when Jiang made his ground-breaking speech, its senior leaders were aware that the CPC was facing a growing crisis of legitimacy. Highly regarded intellectuals, like He Qinliang, Yu Shicun and Sun Liping, had been warning their readers that money and politics had become so inextricably intertwined that it had become impossible to combine growth with social justice; that China was developing not a plural but a fractured society in which the middle class was being crushed between the very rich and the very poor (Fewsmith 2002). Even writers who were more optimistic about China's capacity to meet the political challenges that had been thrown up by its rapid and cadre–initiated development, readily recognized that the problems did exist (ibid).

Officially, the leadership had frowned on these outbursts of criticism. He Qinglian's second book, *We are Watching the Stars Above*, published in June 2001, was banned immediately. Chen Guidi and Wu Juntao's 'Survey of the Life of China's Peasants' was first allowed to be published but then hastily withdrawn and the authors shunned and hounded out of their home town in 2004. But it took the criticism sufficiently seriously to start its own investigation. The result came as a shock. The results of a 'millennium' survey of attitudes of 300,000 party members, carried out in 2000 gave the leaders a huge shock for it showed a high degree of moral decay in the CPC. The only part of the survey's findings that they released to the public was that in Sichuan province, 32 per cent of the party cadres focused exclusively on what their superiors wanted, and not on service to the people. Since this was not, by itself, a shockingly high figure, analysts concluded that the party leaders had been shocked by what they had chosen not to reveal (Fewsmith 2002).[6]

This was only one of a succession of surveys made both before and after it that showed mounting dissatisfaction with the performance of the government and distrust in the party. In 1998, the Central State Council Letters and Visits Office, the highest authority from which citizens could seek redress of their grievances, received 460,000 protests and appeals from the country. Two-thirds came from peasants and were complaints against several types of arbitrary, corrupt and extortionate behaviour by local party cadres (Cai 2003a: 672). A survey of urban residents in 1999 showed that they felt more politically disempowered than they had in 1990. And another nation-wide survey of 2,723 respondents in 2002 showed that the people believed their ability to influence government decisions, to get equal treatment from the government and to get independent judgements from the courts based on law, was only marginally greater than it had been before 1978 (Pei 2006: 4).[7]

Despite serious discomfort in the party, there was no significant response to the rising discontent in the country and animosity towards party cadres so long as Jiang Zemin remained its general secretary. Changes began only after Hu Jintao became the president, in spring 2003. These too took time to unfold. The party's tradition of emphasizing continuity discouraged even a hint of criticism of his predecessor. The composition of its leadership after the 16th Party Congress also left him in no position to take a distinct line of his own. From 1999 the head of the Organisation Department of the Central Committee of the party, and therefore the man responsible for most of the senior postings in the regional and central governments was Zeng Qinghong, a close ally of Jiang Zemin from 1984, when he was the mayor of Shanghai. After the 16th Party Congress, six of the nine members of the Standing Committee of the Politburo, and 12 out of its 15 other members either were recognized supporters of Jiang Zemin or favoured his policies. Zeng Qinhong himself became Hu Jintao's vice-President. Thus, there was no reference to the impending crisis of legitimacy in a speech Hu Jintao gave on the three represents in 2002 (Fewsmith 2003).

Hu's First Moves

But while he made no pronouncements, Hu Jintao and Premier Wen Jiabao unfolded a three-pronged strategy to reform and reshape the party, address the immediate causes of discontent and correct the underlying distortions in the structure of the state and party in which the discontent was ultimately rooted. Within weeks of ascending to the Presidency, he launched a massive drive against corruption in the party and began to show an ostentatious and well-publicized concern for the plight of workers, peasants, the ailing and the destitute.

Senior cadres, who had prospered under the benign neglect of Jiang Zemin, suddenly found themselves being investigated. So fierce was the drive that according to the state-run *Wen Wei Po* daily, 1,252 party members killed themselves, 8,371 absconded and 6,528 disappeared in the first half of 2003. Countless others were given the death penalty or sent to prison (Watts 2004).

Wen Jiabao, then still the vice-Premier, spent New Year's Eve 2003 sharing dumplings with coal miners 500 m below ground in a coal mine. This was the incumbent régime's way of showing that it intended to do something to bring down the extraordinarily high mortality rate in China's coal mines, which had claimed 59,543 lives in a decade between 1992 and 2001, a fatality rate 10 times as high, per million tones of coal mined, as India's and 125 times as high as that of the US (Wright 2004). Eleven months later, Wen became the first Chinese Prime Minister to visit Acquired Immunodeficiency Syndrome (AIDS) patients in a Beijing hospital. He was followed a year later by Hu Jintao himself.[8] Wen Jiabao spent his New Year's Eve, 2005, having dinner with the families of AIDS patients, and a few weeks later on 15 February 2005, Hu Jintao celebrated the Spring Festival, China's most important family reunion, with villagers in an impoverished village in Guizhou province. Wen Jiabao spent the 2005 Spring Festival in a village in Henan province where a large number of blood donors had contracted AIDS from infected needles.[9] Wen Jiabao spent the New Year's Eve 2007 with farmers in Jiangsu, Hu Jintao visited villagers in Hebei a few days earlier (Oon 2007).

Wen Jiabao also prepared the party and the country for the coming changes of policy. In an address delivered to a party meeting in late December 2005, and released in Chinese newspapers 3 weeks later, Wen made a critical admission. 'We absolutely cannot commit a historic error over land problems', he told the assembled delegates. 'In some areas, illegal seizures of farmland without reasonable compensation have provoked uprisings. This is still a key source of instability in rural areas and even the whole society' (Kahn 2006). The Chinese newspapers published this statement less than a month later, on 20 January, in a report that also disclosed that the number of public protests had risen by 13 per cent—to 87,000 in 2005—and the number of incidents in which public order was disturbed by 6.6 per cent.[10] This dispelled any remaining doubt that important changes of domestic policy were in the offing.

Breaking the Hold of the Shanghai Gang

But substantial reform was far from easy. It required first a weakening of the power centres in the party that had fostered, and benefited most from, the growth-first policies of the previous decade, and then the induction of fresh cadres in senior posts who shared his vision and concerns. Hu Jintao unveiled his campaign for taking control of the government and party at the Third Plenary session of the 16th Central Committee, in October 2003. There were three items on the agenda, a work report, some proposed revisions to the constitution and a 'Decision of the CCP Central Committee on Several Issues in Perfecting the Socialist Market Economy'. This was the only document later made public and in a quiet, unemphatic way, it made a complete break with the policies of Jiang Zemin. Whereas the 16th Party Congress the previous year—Jiang Zemin's Last Hurrah—endorsed the target of further quadrupling gross domestic product, the Third Plenum emphasized the need to balance economic with social and cultural development. And whereas the 16th Party Congress report emphasized China's achievements, the Third Plenum focused on the problems that remained: '...the relations of distribution have not been straightened out, rural incomes are increasing slowly, prominent contradictions persist in employment, increasing pressures are emerging from the resource environment, the overall competitiveness of the economy is not strong...' (Fewsmith 2004).

But in implementing them, he faced two interconnected problems: First, most of the social discontent was being generated by the growth of inequality and the flowering of corruption and extortion. But the overwhelming proportion of these sins of commission and omission were being committed by local cadres, ranging from powerful provincial party bosses to millions of township and village cadres, over whom the central government had virtually no control. Hu Jintao's first major decision was to re-establish the central government's control over investment. In the beginning of 2004, he and Wen Jiabao adopted a 'macroeconomic control' policy whose ostensible purpose was to prevent an overheating of the Chinese economy similar to what had occurred in 1993 and 1994 and to avoid 'a financial bubble'. This included sharp increases in the bank rate, physical limits on bank lending, much stricter central oversight over land use and a constant monitoring and limitation of fixed investment in key sectors such as steel, cement and real estate which were showing signs of overheating. But both leaders emphasized that the central government was asking for a slowdown of investment in all sectors and regions of the country. They made it clear that the energy, technology and education sectors were specifically exempted and that they intended increasing state investment in the agriculture, transportation and social welfare sectors, especially in the less-developed western and north-eastern regions (Li 2004: 1).[11]

The city that epitomized defiance of the centre, and had indeed done so since shortly after the Tiananmen crisis, was Shanghai. Ever since Deng Xiaoping decided to develop Pudong, the eastern part of Shanghai, in 1990, Shanghai has been a focal point for modernization in the PRC. Indeed, since the mid-1990s Shanghai has become the showcase for China's coming of age. To finance this grandiose project, Shanghai received a large number of grants and loans from the central government between 1990 and 2002. When Jiang Zemin was the general secretary of the Chinese Communist Party (CCP), Shanghai received 19.8 billion yuan more than did its main domestic competitor, Tianjin.

The deluge of state grants in turn stimulated more foreign direct investment (FDI) in the city. Between 1978 and 2001, 86 per cent of the total FDI in China went to the cities of the eastern coast. By the end of 1999, 144 of the world's 500 largest firms had invested in 511 projects in Shanghai. Another 110 had opened offices there. About 200 foreign banks had opened branches or offices in the city. In 1999, there were some 20,000 foreign investment projects worth a total of $30 billion, financed wholly or partially by FDI. Not surprisingly therefore, after Jiang consolidated his power in the mid-1990s Shanghai experienced the biggest building boom the world had ever seen. According to the Shanghai municipal government, in the early 1990s annual investment in the real estate sector was less than $120 million. In 2001, the figure reached $7.6 billion, 'implying a compound annual growth rate of over 50 percent' during that decade (Li 2004).[12] While there were only three buildings in the city that exceeded 20 stories in height in 1980 and 152 in 1990, there were 1,478 in 2000 and 1,930 in 2003. In the late 1990s, 3 million labourers from the provinces were employed at the city's estimated 21,000 construction sites (Yatsko 2000: 26). A reporter for the *Wall Street Journal* was not entirely exaggerating when he wrote in 1993,

'What's going on in Shanghai, and up and down the China coast, might be the biggest construction project the planet has ever seen since the coral polyps built the Great Barrier Reef after the last Ice Age' (Sterba 1993: 9).

By the mid-1990s Shanghai was showing all the signs of developing a property bubble, but despite the oversupply of floor space, the price of real estate continued to climb. Based on data released by the municipal government, a total of 2 million residents had to be relocated in order to pave the way for property development, including 1 million residents who were moved out of the downtown areas, between 1992 and 1997. But the apartments that were coming up were well out of reach of the ordinary working class. The market they were catering to was of wealthy people, including *nouveaux riches* from other parts of the country and from Hong Kong, Taiwan and Singapore. Much the same thing was happening in the nearby cities in the Yangtze River Delta. In Hangzhou, for example, the average price of new housing increased from 2,000 yuan per sq.m in 1999 to 6,000 yuan per sq.m in 2003. A survey of residents in 11 cities in Zhejiang province showed that 85 per cent could not afford the housing prices in their cities. Small-scale public protests against official corruption, the wrongdoings of real estate companies and the drastic dislocation of downtown residents had become a routine phenomenon in the coastal cities.

The rising dissent acquired political overtones because, in the eyes of a by-now sizable public opinion, Shanghai's miraculous growth was taking place at the expense of other parts of the country. It was therefore the 'head of the dragon'. But Shanghai's party leaders were oblivious of the tide of ill will that was gathering in the party and among the intelligentsia, and remained obsessed with high speed property development. Thus, in 2002 they re-started the construction of the Shanghai Global Financial Center, intended to be the tallest building in the world, which had been halted for 4 years, in the wake of the Asian financial crisis. Mayor Han Zhen told the international media, a few months later, that the Shanghai property boom would surely continue for 'a long time'.

In mid-2003, the Shanghai municipal government decided to offer a series of favourable economic policies to develop its three suburban districts—Songjiang, Jiading and Qingpu. The leaders of these three districts made a 'commitment' to the municipal government that they would build 'three new Pudongs within three years' Inspired by

Shanghai fever, nearby cities such as Suzhou, Kunshan, Hangzhou and Ningbo, all set ambitious goals for economic growth (Li 2004).

Shanghai was one of the main centres, if not the epicentre of the runaway boom that was developing in 2004. It was also the Jiang Zemin faction's power base. So that was where Hu Jintao decided to reassert Beijing's macro-economic control. The central government cancelled 400 billion yuan ($48 billion) worth of projects. These included a theme park, a 40 km undersea tunnel, a horse racing track and several new subway lines. Shanghai was not alone in facing the axe. Beijing also listed 1,000 projects for cancellation in Jiangsu province (also in the Yangtze Delta) including a proposed airport for Suzhou. Zhejiang was made to stop the construction of 19 large steel, cement and aluminium plants and 90 per cent of its planned industrial parks. Beijing also sent investigation teams to the Yangtze Delta to look into charges of illegal acquisition of land and finance to carry out industrial projects (Li 2004).

The party in Shanghai opposed this drive from the very beginning. Its secretary, Chen Liangyu, voiced strong dissent with this policy in the Politburo, at a meeting in June 2004, and accused Wen Jiabao of wanting to harm the interests of the Yangtze River Delta. Citing statistics and projections, he also claimed that putting brakes on investment would hamper future growth. Hu Jintao reportedly came to Wen's defence and rejected Chen's criticism, responding that the Politburo had adopted this macro-economic policy and that all local governments, including Shanghai, should therefore carry it out.

Chen Liangyu also resented and opposed the new leadership's ways of dealing with issues such as the accountability of government officials and the enforcement of measures to curb corruption and punish offenders. When, under pressure from Hu and the Central Disciplinary Inspection Commission (CDIC). Zhou Zhengyi, one of Shanghai's richest real estate tycoons, was arrested and charged with bank stock fraud and illicit property trading; the Shanghai courts sentenced him to only 3-year imprisonment. What is more, the prosecutors carefully skirted what many analysts believed was the real issue in the indictment—the fact that in China, where all land vested in the state, no real estate fraud was possible without the connivance of high government officials. The indictment of Zhou Zhengyi was therefore a veiled accusation against Chen Liangyu for adopting a laisser faire attitude towards corruption. His open attack on the Hu-Wen team at the June 2004 Politburo meeting therefore did not come as a surprise (Li 2004: 5).

An analysis of the speeches given by various leaders during the summer of 2004 showed that Hu Jintao and Wen Jiabao were not enamoured of growth because they were fully aware of the backlash of discontent it tended to create, when the inevitable backlash to uncontrolled investment occurred. The Shanghai leadership, by contrast, had no such worries. Thus, while Wen Jiabao was asking for a continuation of curbs on investment into the second half of 2004, saying that the problem of overheating had not been solved, one of his own vice-premiers, Huang Ju, did not hesitate to assert, at an international seminar in Beijing in May, that the macro-economic controls had already had the desired effect and needed to be relaxed (Li 2004: 5).

Chen Liangyu and the 'Shanghai gang' carried their contempt for Beijing to extraordinary lengths. Chen is reported to have said, 'I have a dream' (French 2007). But unlike Martin Luther King, his dream was not about equality but its opposite. He had set out to make Shanghai the premier city of Asia, if not the world. If this meant making it one of the most inegalitarian cities, he was prepared to pay the price. The deadline he had set himself was the 2010 World Expo, which was to be held in Shanghai. To do so he embarked upon a series of grandiose projects with a royal disregard for costs and returns. The 'hai' in Shanghai, he used to lament, meant the ocean, but Shanghai had no beach. So the government shipped in 128,000 tonnes of sand from southern China to build a 10-km long beach in the suburbs. Not only did Chen Liangyu re-start construction of the world's tallest building, which had been stopped, *soi disant*, after the Asian crisis, but he also commissioned a $290 million, world class tennis complex and a $300 million formula one race track, both consciously designed to be among the most modern and best in the world. It did not matter to him that few Chinese-owned cars, and fewer still played tennis (French 2007). So grandiose was the planning that the race track may have ended by costing $1.24 billion (Kahn 2004).

Chen Liangyu finally overstepped himself when he announced plans to extend a 30 km magnetic levitation train, which linked Shanghai airport to the Pudong economic zone, to Hangzhou. Built at a cost of $1.3 billion and opened for public service in January 2004, the train ranked as one of the biggest white elephants of all time with an estimated payback period, if all went well, of more than 160 years (Callick 2006). Public discontent had been mounting steadily as the Shanghai government raced to complete its basket of mega-projects. Tens of thousands of long-time residents of the central parts had been evicted and re-settled in remote suburbs. Inevitably, rumours of high-level corruption multiplied and fed on themselves. The government's announcement that it intended to extend the Maglev train to Hangzhou at an estimated cost of $5 billion proved to be the last straw. The public protests became so intense and continuous, that Chen's government could not convene without a massive security deployment, worthy of a visit by a foreign head of state.[13]

The rising public discontent gave Hu Jintao the pretext that he needed to break the hold of the Shanghai gang. On 25 September, he dismissed Chen Liangyu from the position of Party Secretary and suspended him from membership of the Central Committee and the Politburo, for possibly having siphoned off funds from a 10 billion yuan Social Security Fund, and sundry associated lesser charges. In May 2007, his pet project—the Maglev extension to Hangzhou—was cancelled, and in July he was stripped of his membership of the Communist Party in preparation for a possible trial. By then, other members of the Shanghai clique, including vice-President Zeng Qinghong and two vice-premiers had already begun to make their peace with Hu Jintao (Li 2004: 9).

Third Rectification of the Party

Breaking the hold of the 'Shanghai Gang' was only half the battle for the reform of the CCP. The other half was to remould it into a party dedicated to serving the people. To do this, Hu Jintao began systematically to replace older retiring members of the Politburo and other bodies with graduates of the China Youth League, the party's youth wing (Li 2006a). He also launched a sustained ideological campaign within the party. On 5 January 2005, The *Peoples' Daily* published a lead editorial blandly titled 'Educational Activities', in which it announced that the CCP was launching a new campaign to re-educate its cadres. The campaign would be mounted in three phases over 18 months. As was their wont in important pronouncements, China's leaders used the editorial to stress a continuity of policy and absence of disagreement within the party. But in fact it heralded a radical shift in the priorities of the Communist Party of China, away from its previous stress on rapid growth at virtually any cost, towards achieving growth with greater equity and social justice.

The ostensible purpose of the campaign was to reorganize the party along the lines sketched out by former President Jiang Zemin in his 'three Represents'. But in reality, it gave the new leadership an opportunity to assess the existing senior cadres at various levels of government and decide whom to reshuffle and replace. The reshuffle began immediately after the 're-education'. In the next 12 months, the party replaced or reshuffled 170,000 senior members of party committees at four levels of government (Li 2006a).

The doors to self-criticism had been opened a little over 3 months earlier, in September, by the Fourth Plenum of the CCP, which had passed a resolution voicing the fear that the party was at a crucial juncture 'at which the ongoing marketization of the economy, the pluralization of social interests, and the intensification of social contradictions have *threatened the ruling status of the party*' (emphasis added) (Fewsmith 2005: 1–10). The *Peoples' Daily*'s editorial, which referred to it, clearly reflected a decision by the leadership to draw the party cadres' and the country's attention to the changes that were imminent. A few days after it appeared, *Xinhua*, China's official news agency, released a news item that left readers in no doubt that a major rectification campaign was in the offing. The news item was captioned 'Opinions of the Chinese Communist Party Central Committee'. It cited 'the abuse of power and the "moral degeneration" of some party cadres, the weakness of many grassroots party organizations, and the inability of some leaders to deal effectively with complex social issues' to be the main threats to its authority. The leaders, it revealed, had resolved to 'improve the education of the cadres, develop inner party democracy and enhance the capacity to govern' (Fewsmith 2005).

By the end of 2004, Hu had sufficiently consolidated his power to start shifting the locus of Chinese politics. In two speeches, on 14 and 24 January 2005, he made it clear that he intended to improve the party's ability to govern, and 'establish the party for the public and government for the people' (Fewsmith 2005: 2).

January also saw the publication by official agencies of data on social unrest in the country. While incidents involving violence and mass demonstrations had been reported with increasing frequency in the media, this was the first time that the state had collected information from across the nation and publicized it. The data came as a shock, for it sowed an exponential growth in discontent, from 10,000 protests in 1994 to 87,000 in 2005. In 2004, more than 3.5 million persons took part in 74,000 protests. Hu Jintao used this information as a launch pad for a shift in the locus of government policy.

Harmonious Society

He announced the change of direction on 19 February 2005. In a highly publicized speech he gave at the Central Committee's Party School, at the opening of a 7-day training course for ministerial and senior provincial level cadres, he said:

> The CPC and the central government have made it an important task to build a harmonious society, which serve(s) the fundamental interests of the people...it was important to balance the interests between different social groups, to avoid conflicts and to make sure people live a safe and happy life in a politically stable country.
>
> A harmonious society will feature democracy, the rule of law, equity, justice, sincerity, amity and vitality. Such a society will give full scope to people's talent and creativity, enable all the people to share the social wealth brought by reform and development, and forge an ever closer relationship between the people and government. These things will result in lasting stability and unity. (*China Daily* 2005a)

The term 'harmonious society was endorsed by the party at its October 2006 plenum, and its content discussed extensively at the National Peoples' Congress (NPC) in March 2007. But it had a mixed reception. Within China, it quickly became an omnibus phrase, used to justify whatever the speaker had in mind. Elsewhere, and particularly in the industrialized countries, several analysts concluded that Hu Jintao was a conservative, partly because he did not come from one of the rich coastal provinces. Others held that he was using populist slogans and gestures to weaken the Jiang Zemin faction in the party leadership. So a few weeks later, the leadership felt it necessary to spell out what it had in mind with greater precision. An editorial opinion in the *China Daily* did so on 12 March 2005:

> A harmonious society includes a slew of elements: democracy, the rule of law, equity and justice, sincerity, amity and vitality.

That calls for an alternative to single-minded pursuit of economic achievement at all costs...In the trade-off between efficiency and equity, our policy-makers have for a long time put more accent on the former. As a result, gross domestic product (GDP) has become an overriding gauge of political achievement. After years of staggering economic growth, China's national strength has ballooned while its social undertakings have fallen way behind.

At the core of the new concept lies the government's commitment to equity on the basis of the rule of law. To that end, it is vital for the government to revamp its governance. A heritage of the planned-economy regime, the government is still sometimes meddling in enterprises' business. Although administrative powers are subject to increasing constraints as the country embraces market-oriented reforms, the government remains a decisive force in allocating resources.

The government needs to make greater efforts to promote social equality by improving social security, employment, medical care, poverty reduction and education. It must especially devise policies to help rural areas develop faster to catch up with better-off urban regions. From the concept of the 'harmonious society', China has begun a long march toward the right choice. (*China Daily Editorial* 2005)

The editorial dispelled whatever doubt remained about Hu Jintao and his Prime Minister Wen Jiabao's intention to shift the emphasis in the party's policies from growth towards equity and social justice.

The party rectification campaign that he launched in 2005 marked his break with the past. The doors to self-criticism had been opened a little over 3 months earlier, in September, by the Fourth Plenum of the CCP, which had passed a resolution voicing the fear that the party was at a crucial juncture; it is reflected in Fewsmith words, 'at which the ongoing marketization of the economy, the pluralization of social interests and the intensification of social contradictions have *threatened the ruling status of the party*' (emphasis added) (2005). The *Peoples' Daily*'s editorial, which referred to it, clearly reflected a decision by the leadership to draw the party cadres' and the country's attention to the changes that were imminent. A few days after it appeared, *Xinhua*, China's official news agency, released a news item that left readers in no doubt that a major rectification campaign was in the offing. The news item was captioned 'Opinions of the Chinese Communist Party Central Committee'. It cited 'the abuse of power and the "moral degeneration" of some party cadres, the weakness of many grassroot party organizations, and the inability of some leaders to deal effectively with complex social issues, to be the main threats to its authority. The leaders, it revealed, had resolved to 'improve the education of the cadres, develop inner party democracy and enhance the capacity to govern' (Fewsmith 2005).

Dual Purpose of Tax-for-fee Reform

Many analysts have compared the downfall of Chen Liangyu with that of Chen Xitong, the mayor of Beijing, a decade earlier. Chen Xitong had been stripped of power and accused of relatively vague charges by Jiang Zemin, in what had been widely perceived then as Jiang's bid to consolidate his, and Shanghai's, power at the centre. Hu was accused of having done the same in reverse. But breaking the power of Shanghai was only a part, albeit a crucially important one, of a much broader strategy to restore the legitimacy and authority of the Communist Party. Hu was well aware of the fact that nearly all the discontent was being triggered by the actions of local government officials and party cadres. These included the seizure of land, the extraction of arbitrary and extortionate local taxes and fees, and a brutal use of force to discourage villagers and other victims from taking the matter up to higher levels of party and government (Li 2006b). Hu therefore decided to restore legitimacy of central authority by stripping the local governments of the powers that they were abusing in their dealings with the rural population. Most of the reforms that they enacted therefore had a dual purpose—to relieve the immediate burden on the rural population and to strip the local governments, particularly at the township and village-level, of the powers to tax and invest, that they had previously enjoyed.

The most drastic of these reforms, enacted in stages between 2004 and 2006 were the tax-for-fee reform (TFR), and the abolition of the agricultural tax.

The TFR was intended to plug the loopholes that local governments had exploited in the 1994 tax reforms to continue taxing the peasants. First tried out in Anhui in 2000, and extended to 20 provinces on an experimental basis in 2002, it replaced the multitude of fees, often illegal and arbitrary, that local authorities were levying on the peasantry, with a single tax of 5 per cent on agricultural cash crops other than tobacco. It had two goals. The first was to reduce the burden of levies on the rural population. The second was to force the local governments to reduce their bloated bureaucracies in the face of hard budget constraints. According to newspaper reports, it dramatically reduced the exactions from the peasants (China Daily 2005b). But a more fundamental restructuring of centre–province financial relations, soon overtook the TFR.

In 2004, the Yan-an municipal district in the province of Shaanxi, which had been among the first to introduce the TFR, went a step further and also abolished the agricultural tax and the agricultural specialties tax, in short all taxes on agriculture. The central government took this opportunity to announce the elimination of agricultural taxation in 5 years, but brought this forward by 3 years to the beginning of 2006 (Kennedy 2007).

The central government decided to advance the schedule because by 2004, the yield of the agricultural taxes had become insignificant.[14] The taxes were steeply regressive, for their impact was most severe on the poorest families in each village on the poorest villages and in the least industrialized parts of the country. They were also difficult, and therefore expensive, to collect. Finally, the booming economy was filling the coffers of the central and provincial governments from other sources steeply regressive, for its impact was most severe on the poorest families in each village, and on the poorest villages in the least industrialized parts of the country (Wu 2005).[15]

The agriculture taxes were abolished so soon after the TFR was implemented that it is difficult to separate the social impact of one from the other. According to official reports, the number of public disturbances also fell for the first time in more than a decade. This is indirectly confirmed by the fact that large numbers of seasonal migrant workers who went back to their farms in 2006 did not return for work to the city. This should not have come as a surprise, because surveys had shown that by the early years of the current decade, the conditions of the migrant workers in the cities had deteriorated to the point where they were worse off than those who had been able to find non-agricultural work in their home counties (Guang and Zheng 2005). This caused a sudden and unexpected shortage of labour in many industrial towns (Chung-Yan 2005).[16]

The TFR has also, to a considerable extent, achieved its second purpose—of downsizing the rural administration (Kennedy 2007). But studies conducted in Shaanxi suggest that it was not an unmixed blessing. On the one hand, the relief felt by the peasants is palpable. But on the other, there is a substantial amount of evidence that Beijing has tried to compensate for the abolition of both taxes and fees by transferring money directly to the counties to meet a part of the townships and villages' education, health and infrastructural expenses.[17] In February 2006, Wen Jiabao announced that the centre would transfer 100 billion yuan directly to the county and lower-levels of provincial administration to compensate for the abolition of fees and waiver of the agriculture tax.[18] This is one of a slew of measures endorsed by the NPC in March 2006. They included a promise to spend an overall 340 billion yuan on rural health, education and infrastructure (14 per cent more than in the previous year) (Hon 2006);[19] an exemption from the income tax for anyone earning less than 1,600 yuan for month and, most significantly, a strict ban on local governments, expropriating peasants and assigning land to industry at throwaway prices or free of cost.

Once the party had officially endorsed the goal of creating a 'Harmonious Society', Hu and Wen embarked upon other, substantial, urban and rural reforms. The most important of these was a decision to guarantee rights of usage of their land for 30 years.[20] This has paved the way for a pilot project in Guangdong province by which the tillers of the land, whose land was transferred to non-agricultural use, would receive a part of the price. If this is implemented nationwide, it will turn former victims into stakeholders in development (Callick 2007).[21] The government also committed itself to abolishing school fees in rural areas in 2007.[22]

In June 2007, the Standing Committee of the NPC passed a new labour law that would allow trade unions to engage in collective bargaining for the first time. It also required enterprises that laid-off workers to 'consult' with the unions first.[23] From 2006, the unions began to recruit 8 million more migrant workers every year. In 2006, they were expected to exceed this figure and increase the unionized migrant labour force to 33.5 million.[24]

But the experience of Yan-an suggests that the TFR too may at best provide temporary relief, because it has not solved the core problem that local governments have faced since 1994. This is what Chen Guidi and Wu Chuntao described as the 'upward movement of revenues and downward movement of responsibilities'.[25] As was described earlier, the 1994 reforms plunged townships, town and village administrations into a financial crisis. They had tried to make ends meet by levying an ever expanding list of fees and administrative charges and by borrowing ever more heavily from banks and rural credit institutions. Practically, all the extortionate impositions upon the peasants described in the last chapter sprang from the effort to cut the same coat (with silken lining of course) out of a smaller amount of cloth.

By taking away most of not all revenue-raising powers, the TFR has made this problem more, not less acute. In the more industrialized counties, this problem has been hidden for the time being by the surge in tax revenues caused by the economic boom. But as happened in 1997, it will rebound on them when the boom turns into recession, profits turn into losses and revenues dry up. The poorer provinces and the relatively un-industrialized counties do not have even this reprieve. The Party Secretary of a township in Yan-an told a researcher that minus the agriculture taxes, its revenues were only 30,000 yuan, but its expenses were 200,000 yuan. On an average, in the poorer counties, the two agricultural taxes used to contribute 30 per cent of the total revenue (Kennedy 2007: 56).

Beijing has tried to compensate for the abolition of both taxes and fees by transferring money directly to the counties, to meet a part of the townships and villages' education, health and infrastructure expenses.[26] In February 2006, Wen Jiabao announced that the centre would transfer 100 billion yuan directly to the county and lower levels of provincial administration to compensate for the abolition of fees and waiver of the agriculture tax.[27] This is one of a slew of measures endorsed by the NPC in March 2006. They included a promise to spend an overall 340 billion yuan on rural health, education and infrastructure (14 per cent more than in the previous year);[28] an exemption from the income tax for anyone earning less than 1,600 yuan for month and, most significantly, a strict ban on local governments expropriating peasants and assigning land to industry at throwaway prices or free of cost.

But the experience of Shaanxi suggests that as happened in 1994, these 'transfer payments' will not come close to meeting the townships' needs. A survey carried out in 2002 by the State Council's Development Research Centre revealed that village committees were raising 78 per cent of the total cost of education, while the county, provincial and central administrations together met only 22 per cent. If, as estimated by Minchin Pei, 85 per cent of the village committees' contribution came from off-budget revenues, collected as administrative fees and levies, the gap that would be left by abolishing both fees and taxes can only be filled by quadrupling the transfers to them from the centre, province and county.[29] The transfers announced in 2006 have not come close to filling this gap (Kennedy 2007: 49). The reason is that, while the counties paid the salaries of primary school teachers from 2001, the township administrations were responsible for building the schools, maintaining them and meeting the cost of living allowances of the teachers. These, as well as health services, used to be met through five basic fees (which multiplied as the financial crisis deepened). As a result of the TFR, the villages and townships no longer had sufficient funds to meet these costs. By 2003, the number of students had declined by 24 per cent and the number of schools by 15 per cent (Kennedy 2007: 51).

The reforms also forced the local administration to cut back on the already meagre health benefits that the rural population enjoyed. As medical out-of-pocket expenses soared through the 1990s, more and more people had come to rely upon the health care workers and rural doctors, employed by the township and village administrations. After the reforms, these lost their capacity to pay. As a result, there was an 82 per cent decrease in health workers in Shaanxi province from 15,365 to 2,813, and a 23 per cent reduction in the number of doctors from 27,718 to 28,401 (Kennedy 2007: 53–54). The reforms also forced the township and village administrations to cut back on three other important subsidies—housing, coal and grain. Kennedy's research in Shaanxi therefore confirmed the fears voiced by Ray Yap in 2003–04, that while the abolition of the right to levy fees would bring a great deal of relief to the peasants, it would also impair their ability to provide essential services. Even where the greater control of the county and prefectural administrations led to a net improvement in these services—a possibility not ruled out by either Yep or Kennedy—it would reduce the autonomy of lower levels of local administration and, particularly in the poorer provinces, turn the township and village administrations into mere shells (Yap 2004).

A Bunch of Half Measures

Hu Jintao and Wen Jiabao's campaign to create a 'new Socialist countryside' is still gathering momentum, so it is too early to predict how effective it will be. But it is difficult to resist the suspicion that all he is doing is applying poultice to an open sore instead of treating the infection. All the measures described above are, in the end, half measures.

- The TFR, the subsequent abolition of the agriculture taxes is providing immediate relief. The proposed abolition of school fees in the rural areas will provide still more. But these will make the townships and villages completely dependent upon transfers from the provincial and county governments. The struggle by them to corner resources will therefore remain dormant only so long as the economy is enjoying a boom and the provincial revenues are rising rapidly. It will begin once again the moment boom turns into recession, as happened in 1997.
- The new property law, unveiled at the March 2007 meeting of the NPC, was even more blatantly a half measure. While it gave 30-year leasehold rights to farmers, it rejected the proposal to transfer full ownership rights to them (Queck 2007). It did not therefore significantly reduce the right of the local branches of the party to take over their land at short notice, in exchange for a compensation from which they have, so far, been appropriated— up to 90 per cent—to meet various 'expenses'.
- The right of collective bargaining granted to trade unions only requires enterprises to *consult* with the unions, and not, as some reformers had proposed, to obtain their consent. And even the 33 million unionized migrant workers, at the end of 2006, made up only a sixth of the total number of such workers. Five-sixths remained outside the fold, and their numbers were slated to grow for, while the unions were mandated to recruit 8 million more workers every year, the number of migrant workers was estimated to be growing by 13 million.[30]
- Under Hu Jintao, the central government has not only maintained but also tightened its control on Internet. Hu Jintao declared his intention to 'purify' the Internet, in a front page article in the *Peoples' Daily* (Coonan 2007). He made this statement during a discussion among senior party leaders on ways to keep China's Internet community in check. 'Whether we can cope with the internet is a matter that affects the development of socialist culture, the security of information and the stability of the state', Mr Hu said.

Scattered reports from the countryside suggest that while there has been a decline in the number of protests, those that are taking place have become larger, more prolonged and more violent. What is more, the abuse of power by the party cadres is not proving easy to uproot. The following examples show how little has actually changed so far in the rural areas:

- In October 2004, more than 10,000 farmers who were facing relocation because of a new dam in Ya'an, Sichuan, took out a demonstration. Nervous authorities called in the Peoples' Armed Police. The resulting clashes led to the deaths of at least, one protester and two policemen.
- In April 2005, 20,000 peasants from several villages in Huaxi township, Zhejiang province, who had been complaining for 4 years of industrial pollution from an industrial park that had ruined their agricultural livelihood, fought with police. Before the protests, local elected village councils and the township Communist Party Secretary had made futile pleas to higher authorities to respond to the peasants' concerns. The factories were eventually shut down but the protest leaders were arrested.
- In June 2005, about 100 miles south-west of Beijing, approximately 300 hired thugs attacked a group of farmers who had camped on disputed land that the local government had planned to use to build a power plant. The farmers protested the lack of proper compensation for their land. Six villagers reportedly were killed in the attack, which was captured on video by a protester and shown on Chinese websites. The central government fired the local party chief and mayor and returned the farmland.
- In July 2005, residents of Taishi village, near Guangzhou, capital of Guangdong province, submitted a petition to remove their village chief for plundering public funds. After one of their leaders was arrested, 1,500 villagers clashed with 500 armed police. In September 2005, police seized government documents that villagers had been guarding to use in their legal case, alleging official corruption, and shut down an Internet website, that had been reporting on the unrest. Also in July 2005, farmers in Xinchang, 200 km south of Shanghai, attacked a pharmaceutical plant because of anger and lack of redress over pollution, that it emitted.

- In the same month, police beat villagers protesting against pollution from a battery factory in Zhejiang province.
- In August 2005, unemployed residents of Daye, Hubei province, attacked government offices and destroyed cars, after police used dogs to break up a demonstration over an official plan to annex Daye to a larger city, Huangshi. In September 2005, a Chinese court sentenced 10 persons to prison terms, ranging from 1 to 5 years for their involvement in the protests.
- In December 2005, a dispute over the construction of an electricity generating plant and related property seizures culminated in a violent clash in Dongzhou village near Shanwei city, Guangdong province, in which 3–20 demonstrators were killed. Beijing suspended the deputy police chief of Shanwei, restricted movement in and out of the area, imposed a news blackout, and arrested three protest leaders. The year-long conflict included villagers filing formal complaints, setting up roadblocks, and kidnapping local officials; government officials visiting Dongzhou; local authorities detaining and releasing village leaders; and the mysterious death of a village accountant who had supported the farmers' demands.
- In January 2006, hundreds or thousands of protesters clashed with police over inadequate compensation for farmland taken for industrial use in Panlong village, Sanjiao township, Guangdong province. A teenage girl reportedly was killed.[31]
- In March 2006, protest leader Feng Quisheng lost an election bid for the township People's Congress. His supporters claimed that Feng's opponent engaged in vote buying and that proxy votes were not accepted.
- In October 2006, as many as 10,000 students marched through the campus of a vocational college in Nanchang, the capital of Jiangxi province, after they heard reports in the state-run media that the college had deceived new students about their eventual qualification and had issued fake diplomas (Macartney 2006).
- In May 2007, an attempt by the local government to enforce strict population control by forcing women to have abortions sparked a violent clash between villagers and local police in Bobai county of the Guangxi autonomous region of southwestern China. Local officials resorted to compulsory abortion to meet targets set by their superiors. This was done after punitive fines, labelled a 'social child raising fee', ranging from 500 to

70,000 yuan had failed to bring down illegal births sufficiently. The new 'fee' was imposed on families that had already paid an earlier fine for the violation of the birth control rules.

When families objected strongly to the fee and refused to pay, witnesses said, they were detained, their homes searched and valuables, including electronic items and motorcycles, were confiscated by the government. 'Worst of all, the gangsters used hammers and iron rods to destroy people's homes, while threatening that the next time it would be with bulldozers,' said a peasant who identified himself as Nong Sheng, in a letter faxed to a reporter in Beijing. According to reports posted on the internet as many as five persons, including three officials engaged in overseeing population control, were killed in the rioting, which went on for 4 days. Officials in Guangxi in the meantime boasted that they had collected 7.8 million yuan in 'social child-raising fees' between February and the end of April (Kahn 2007).

- In the single month of July 2007 in Chongqing, rioters took to the streets three times. In the third riot, early in July an estimated 5,000 persons participated, and went on a rampage that lasted for more than 2 days, killing one man and injuring 10 others. The unrest began when villagers found that the government was offering three times as much by way of compensation for the extension of an industrial zone as they had received, 3 years earlier. What triggered the riot was their conviction that corruption had lain behind the low prices they had received 3 years earlier. The government shipped in a thousand policemen to put it down (Chan 2007).

- In the same month, 5,000 peasants clashed with the police in Shifang city in Sichuan, because effluents from a privatized brewery, they claimed, had halved their harvest.[32]

These brief descriptions do not, however, capture the full depth of the desperation being felt by peasants, as they see their land gobbled up by factories, residences and golf courses. Nor do they tell us much about the kinds of resistance that the villagers have tried to mount, and the increasingly violent methods that some local authorities have been using to try and keep the dispute local, and therefore outside Beijing's ken. The following eyewitness account of a sustained mass protest in Taishi, one of several large protests mentioned above, that have occurred in the Pearl River Delta in Guangdong, demonstrates vividly how villagers are asserting their rights and confronting the authorities and how, inch by inch, the provincial authorities are losing the battle to isolate them from other aggrieved members of their class. It shows how villagers are gaining support from an infant civil society, consisting of 'barefoot lyres', educated villagers, ex-servicemen and, perhaps most important of all, disillusioned members of the Communist Party itself. The members of this civil society keep in touch with each other and spread information through mobile telephones and the Internet. Their growing success in linking up with villagers, who have been similarly dispossessed is creating the first elements of a class of 'have nots' in Chinese society.

Taishi

In October 2005, Lu Banglie, a social activist in Guangdong, who had been helping villagers to assert their rights was dragged out of a car when he arrived at a village called Taishi, beaten till he was unconscious, and left on the roadside. Journalists of the *Guardian*, who were with him, escaped by taking to the fields. Six weeks later, Edward Cody of the Washington Post pieced together the full story of what had led to the brutal assault.[33]

Construction cranes and factories have increasingly encroached on the banana plots and rice paddies that for centuries had underpinned the economy of the village of Taishi and the surrounding district. The metropolis of Guangzhou, capital of the Pearl River Delta's booming manufacturing region, has swallowed up the rural surroundings. Taishi, with just over 2,000 residents, benefited from the development along with the rest of south-eastern China. The village administration took in $600,000 last year, triple its income of 2001. Each adult received about $100 in dividends from communal village land, given over to factories assembling jewellery, clothing, shoes and electronic components.

But two villagers, Feng Qiusheng and Liang Shusheng, began asking last May why the annual payments were not higher and why the village was deeply in debt. They demanded that Chen, the Party Secretary who had just taken over as village chief, open the accounts. Feng, 26, an accountant, wanted to go over the books himself. But Chen rejected that idea, along with the rest of their questions.

In July, a new face showed up in Guangzhou, the huge nearby metropolis. He was Yang Maodong, a former philosophy professor and an experienced activist. Yang, a stocky, dishevelled intellectual who spoke with rapid-fire intensity and wore the Chinese academic's traditional black-plastic-framed glasses, was a contributor to dissident websites; he had also written a book on the collapse of the Soviet Union. His political beliefs harked back to the democracy spirit of the Tiananmen Square protests in 1989. A natural organizer and unabashed nationalist, he had last been detained in April, for his role in promoting anti-Japanese demonstrations in Beijing. Given his background, it was not long before Yang made a connection with the angry peasants, including Feng, the young accountant who was challenging Chen's leadership of the village.

At a dinner in July organized by Yang in an inexpensive Guangzhou restaurant, Feng was also introduced to Lu, the peasant organizer who was later to be beaten. Lu was already gaining recognition for his activism. In 2003, he had endured beatings and used a 5-day hunger strike to force out the leader of his own village, in Hubei province, on corruption charges. The government run *China Youth Daily* had hailed him at that time as a 'frontrunner of peasant grassroots democracy'. Eager to pursue his activism, he was immediately attracted to the fight over Taishi's leadership.

Lu, whose oily hair and ill-fitting black suit bespeak his peasant background, said he had come to Beijing in April and again in early July, seeking guidance from more educated political activists about what to do next. One of the people he met during those consultations in the capital, he said in an interview, was Yang and the subject of Taishi was already part of their conversation.

An activist leader, speaking on condition of anonymity, said Beijing-based community organizers had decided to lend support to Feng's cause soon after they heard of his challenge. For them, encouraging farmers to push for more democratic village elections was a long-time national goal, and Taishi seemed to fit the bill. They also reasoned this fast-growing region would be fertile ground, he said, because of its economic development and nearness to the relatively liberal atmosphere of Hong Kong.

Lu, the peasant organizer, moved to Guangzhou soon after talking with Yang. He found a job for about $65 a month in a factory, manufacturing plastic Christmas trees. Although he also needed to earn some money, his main motive for moving there was to be on hand to offer advice when the two peasants, Feng and Liang, decided to press a legal case for removing the village leader in Taishi.

Yang and Lu, two veteran activists, quietly got involved in the struggle. They advised the Taishi villagers on what options were open to them under China's election laws; Lu said, and inspired them by recounting Lu's experience in booting out a corrupt leader back home in Hubei province. Basing their demand on the election law and its recall provision, Feng and Liang filed a formal recall motion on 29 July. According to Lu and the district government, the motion was drafted with the help from Lu and Yang. It carried more than 400 signatures, and therefore met the requirement of being endorsed by 20 percent of Taishi's 1,500 registered voters.

Villagers gathered two days later in an open square. From atop a heap of bricks, as local reporters and other witnesses looked on, Feng read a section from Chinese law books saying village accounts must be published every 6 months and villagers had the right to recall Chen. 'The law will be our guardian', he vowed. An alarm bell rang in the village committee office on the evening of 3 August. Villagers who heard the noise rushed to the scene and, they recalled, surprised the village accountant and a companion in what looked like an attempt to spirit away the ledgers. Before the two could get away with the books, the villagers told reporters, a crowd gathered and prevented them from leaving. The accounts stayed put. The next morning, police and district officials came to take the books away—to protect them, they said. Villagers called the Guangzhou Communist Party Discipline and Inspection Bureau, denouncing what they interpreted as an attempt to cover up malfeasance. But their calls elicited no response, they said. A group of elderly women moved into the three-story administration building and refused to budge. The ledgers would stay, they vowed.

As the sit-in continued, plainclothes security agents detained a protest leader as he rode his motorcycle down a village lane on 16 August. On hearing the news, hundreds of villagers poured out of their homes and surrounded the van into which the agents had stuffed the leader, blocking its passage.

After a several-hour confrontation during which the number of protesters swelled to more than 1,000. Witnesses said, an estimated 500 riot police drove up in several dozen vehicles and waded into the crowd, swinging their batons. In internet postings, villagers reported five of their members were arrested. A 16-year-old youth suffered a concussion, they said, and an 80-year-old peasant woman suffered a broken bone and had to be hospitalized. The sit-in continued, meanwhile, with the elderly women still refusing to leave. Within days, their numbers grew.

The district government 2 weeks later handed down a ruling that the recall motion was unacceptable because it was a photocopy, and the law demanded the original signatures. Outraged, a number of villagers, including elderly women, started a hunger strike outside the district headquarters building.

After several days, some of the hunger strikers were detained and later released on condition they return home, the protesters said. As they left custody about 3 p.m., they reported, officials gave them box lunches. Despite the gesture, the atmosphere remained tense. As police moved in to make the arrests, one elderly woman threatened to blow up the building by igniting a canister of liquefied gas, according to witnesses. Yang sent messages to Chinese and foreign reporters recounting what was happening and urging them to visit. A reporter from the Hong Kong-based *South China Morning Post* showed up, and two youths smashed her car windows with rocks.

From that point on, things moved fast. On 5 September, a delegation of villagers went to the district headquarters to present the original recall motion with the original signatures. But official patience had frayed. Activists later speculated that word had come down from Beijing that the uproar in Taishi—and the confluence of political activism with peasant outrage—had to be stopped. Although his role could not be determined, Premier Wen Jiabao visited the region from 9 to 13 September to confer with senior regional and city officials.

Beijing-based activists said they received warnings from the Civil Affairs Ministry about that time to back away from the Taishi dispute. 'Everybody was scared', one of them recalled. Back in Taishi, more than 50 vehicles drove up to the village administration building on 12 September and disgorged hundreds of riot police, witnesses said. Swinging batons and training high pressure hoses on the elderly women inside, the police cleared the building and made way for district officials to take away the account books.

Nearly 50 protesters were taken into custody. The next day, Yang was also arrested as he drove to meet a crew from the Hong Kong-based Phoenix satellite television channel. Lu was urged to leave, but refused. 'You know, he is just like a farmer; he is stubborn', said an activist who has worked with Lu.

Then, in a surprise turn of events, the district government announced that the recall motion has been proven valid and villagers should choose an election committee to organize a new vote for village chief, scheduled for the middle of October. The protests should now stop, it said, and activists with 'ulterior motives' should be ignored.

On first glance, this seemed like a triumph for the villagers. The official party newspaper, *People's Daily*, hailed the outcome as a model for village elections and pointed to signs of 'a democratic environment built upon rationality and legality'. But then the district government arbitrarily chose all candidates for the seven-person election committee—and all were local officials loyal to Chen. Outraged, the still-defiant villagers threatened to boycott the vote. Seeking to prevent more violence, the district government swiftly relented and allowed another slate to run as well.

The vote was held on 16 September; all the unofficial candidates were elected and none of the government's slate. The seven committee members now had 4 weeks to organize a new vote for village chief. But somewhere in the government and party bureaucracy—activists believe it was at a senior level in Beijing—officials had decided Chen would not be replaced, lest a precedent be set.

Lu, who was in the village to monitor the 16 September vote, was picked up by police the same day. After a long interrogation and a warning to clear out of the area, he was released that evening. In what they hoped was a farewell gesture, police officers bought him a pair of $12 shoes, he said later, to replace those that had come off during a brief struggle when he was taken into custody. District officials announced, shortly after the new election committee was chosen, that their auditors had found no evidence of wrongdoing in the Taishi accounts. Party and government officials swiftly fanned out to persuade villagers to drop the struggle. Unless the recall motion was withdrawn, they suggested, detained relatives might stay in jail and people might lose their jobs. The threats worked. The district government reported by the end of September that 396 of the 584 signatures were withdrawn. The recall procedure therefore was invalid, it announced and the vote scheduled for October was cancelled.

Then guards wearing camouflage fatigues, but without official insignia, took up positions at streets leading into the village and began screening outsiders trying to enter and villagers trying to leave. Villagers told activists the guards were unemployed men from surrounding villages paid $12 a day by Chen's head of security. The district government claimed in a statement that they were Taishi villagers upset at the uproar in their community. Two foreign reporters who drove up on 7 October to find out why the signatures were withdrawn were attacked by the guards and driven off.

It was the next night that Lu tried to drive in, along with a reporter from the *Guardian* newspaper, also seeking to learn what had changed since mid-September. ...By the time Lu Banglie drove toward the village of Taishi that night, his photograph had already been distributed to local police stations. So when camouflage-clad men guarding the village entrance stopped his taxi and peered inside, Lu recalled, they immediately shouted, 'It's him! It's him!' and yanked him out by the hair. After dragging him to the side of the street, the guards set on Lu, kicking him and punching him until he passed out, according to Lu and his companions. When Lu regained consciousness more than two hours later, he said, his body was bruised and hurting, his clothing smelled of urine, he was vomiting repeatedly, his vision was blurred and his memory had gone fuzzy.

'We never imagined that we would be suppressed like this', Lu said in an interview nearly two weeks after his beating. Lu's lips were covered with scabs and his arms with bruises. His eyes were blurry at times and his head ached, but he vowed to persist in organizing farmers to pick their own village leaders. 'I will definitely continue', he said, 'but how to do it is the question now'.

11

The Challenge Ahead

China can become the world's largest economy by 2050 as the BRICs report has predicted, but only if it traverses the next 42 years without mishap first. The story of China's growth narrated in the previous chapters suggests that this cannot be taken for granted. Nor does it suggest that China will not make it. It differs in significant respects from the one that has been told by liberal economists, who see in China's transformation a vindication of all their theories about the efficacy of the market. But it also differs from the one being told by a growing number of political scientists, who expect growth to falter because the country is too deeply mired in a corrupt and oppressive political system, to be able to make the transition to democracy that is necessary to sustain and stabilize a market economy. China's growth has been impressive, even phenomenal, but it has not been as fast as the official data make it out to be. The self-reporting system upon which Chinese statisticians still mainly rely, and the increasing politicization of the data on gross domestic product (GDP) growth after 1996, has led to an overestimation of growth, especially during periods of slowdown or recession. All things considered, China's rate of growth during the past three decades has probably been higher than the 7.8 per cent calculated by Angus Maddison, but considerably lower than the 9.8 per cent claimed by the National Bureau of Statistics. All in all, the World Bank's 1998 estimate of an 8.2 per cent rate of growth does not seem too wide off the mark.

This is still a higher average rate of growth than that attained by Japan and the East Asian tigers, and has been maintained for much longer. But there are few lessons to learn from it because it is a product of conditions that are specific to that country that cannot be duplicated, elsewhere. The most important of these is that China's growth has been propelled neither by privatization nor by the increase in efficiency that accompanies the shift from a command to a market economy, but by a hasty and largely unplanned devolution of decision-making power from the central government in Beijing to four subordinate levels of the government at the province/municipality, the prefecture, the county and the township levels. This has given rise to competition between the central and provincial levels of the communist bureaucracy in capturing investable resources, as to who will be the first to invest. The devolution of power took place in stages between 1980 and 1984. It is not surprising therefore that the huge spurt of investment that took growth rates up to the dizzy heights of 12 and 14 per cent in the mid-1980s and again in the mid-1990s, began in 1981.

The period between 1981 and 1995 saw a huge increase in the number of enterprises, all of which were free from the crippling price and distribution controls, as also obligations towards their workers that weighed down the state-owned enterprises of the communist era. But almost none of the new enterprises were privately owned, and literally none were subject to the discipline of the market. While the central government was struggling to reduce the number of state-owned enterprises, the provincial levels established 7.87 million new enterprises.

Corruption was a Siamese twin of decentralization and relaxation of social control. The local bureaucracy raced to invest, and kept investing, not only in order to impress their superiors in the party but also to line their own pockets. China has therefore developed not free enterprise, but a special brand of State capitalism. The Communist Party has emerged as the *de facto* owner of all the property of the state, and therefore as the new propertied class of the country. But this propertied class is no longer united. Instead it is split between a 'High' stratum, the central party leadership, and an 'intermediate' stratum, which is composed of the various levels of local government.

Competition between these two strata to pre-empt the available resources of the country for their projects is therefore the driving force behind China's phenomenal growth. But this investment is based entirely upon success in cornering resources and is insensitive to signals from the market. This accounts for the three most striking features of China's development: the massive duplication of investment and consequently the periodic development of huge surplus capacities;

the frequent adoption, in more complex industries, of sub-optimal scales of production and relatively obsolete technologies; and the wastefulness of its development, measured by its consumption of raw materials and energy per dollar of GDP.

But if China's growth has been slower than estimated and has also been wasteful, how does one account for its stellar performance in exports, its trillion dollar foreign exchange reserves, and its domination of the global market for mass consumption goods?

The answer lies in the development of 'dualism' in the economy. Since it embraced the market, China has become a stellar example of the dual economy that was described four decades ago by Andre Gunder Frank, Samir Amin and others. Its export sector is large, and highly efficient. But the reason is that this is the only sector that is subject fully to the discipline of the market, and that too in its most rigorous form. Of the exports, more than half comes from foreign and joint ventures in China. In addition to their knowledge of the international market, these brought cutting-edge technology and management skills that have been honed in the world market. The rest of the economy, which accounts for 66 per cent of the GDP, is not subject to this discipline. Since the Chinese economy now enjoys very little overt protection, low inefficiency in the basic and intermediate goods and service industries are reflected either by lower wage rates or by accumulating losses that have, periodically, to be written off. The frequent bale-outs of the banking sector provide an approximate yardstick of this indirect subsidy to industry.

The efficiency of the export sector is therefore an indication of what the Chinese economy is capable of if it brings all sectors of the economy fully under the writ of the market. But the hurdles to this are political, rooted in a determination to retain decision-making power in the hands of the state and to accumulate personal wealth through its discretionary use in favour of selected investors. Despite the punishment of up to 200,000 party cadres every year on charges of corruption, these hurdles have shown no sign of becoming any smaller. Thus, the widely held assumption that cadre capitalism will eventually give way to the genuine article, as China completes its transition to the market, remains an extrapolation from the experience of other countries and has little empirical foundation in the developments of the past two decades. On the contrary, political scientists, like Minchin Pei, are much closer to the mark when they say that China is likely to remain trapped in an incomplete transition.

Since growth has been propelled by what are essentially two competing strata of the Chinese State, it has not only been wasteful but also notoriously uneven. This too is in stark contrast to the commonly held belief that China has found a way to defeat the trade cycle. In the past 30 years, China has experienced three prolonged industrial booms and two recessions. The first recession occurred in 1989 and 1990, when GDP growth came abruptly down to 4.2 per cent. The common belief is that this was a by-product of the crackdown at Tiananmen in June 1989, but the economy had begun to descend into a recession when the disturbances occurred. In fact, the student unrest spread to the industrial workers and the *shimin* in Beijing and other cities so rapidly because inflation had reached a peak, and was cutting cruelly into real incomes just when the economy had begun to slacken. This had made industrial workers feel insecure about their future incomes and living standards for the first time since the communist revolution.

The second downswing began at the end of 1995, more than 2 years before Prime Minister Zhu Rongji sounded the warning that 'attaining a seven percent rate of growth (in 1998) would not be easy'. It continued virtually till the end of 2001. The third is imminent: unsold stocks of steel, cement and automobiles began to mount at the end of 2006. As past experience has shown, precisely because the investment booms are not moderated by market forces, the descent into recession is also correspondingly swift. Only the systematic fudging of official GDP data, and their uncritical acceptance by the academic community abroad, has prevented the outside world from getting to know the full depth of the 1996–2001 recession, and the hardship it inflicted on the rural and urban poor.

Recession sharpens class conflict in all industrializing countries. China is no exception. Beginning with the tax reforms of 1994, the central government took a succession of steps in the second half of the 1990s to wrest back control of the resources that the local governments had pre-empted with their plethora of small and medium-sized investments. To lock in its control of these resources it committed them to a large number of mega-projects in central and western China and in the revival of the rusting industrial heartland of the communist era, in the north-east. This has had a number of beneficial effects, among which is an amelioration of the recession in the late 1990s. But it has sharply increased the energy and materials intensity of growth in China and reduced the rate of growth of employment.

Today China is plagued by overt unemployment and, despite several years of rapid growth, its migrant labour force—the equivalent of India's non-agricultural unorganized sector— remains in considerable distress.

When the central government wrested resources back from the local governments, it left the latter with no option but to put the squeeze on the rural peasantry. This was because, while the 1994 tax reforms reduced the share of the provinces in the total tax revenues by a third, it made no corresponding reduction in their administrative duties. As recession deepened and more and more of the TVEs began to incur loses, the township and village administrations found their revenues from the TVEs also drying up. In desperation, they 'sold off' the loss-making enterprises to their workers and managers, often under duress. They also raised loans from the local branches of the four national banks, until the centre took away their power to set up rural credit funds and freed the bank managers from the control of the local party secretary. Finally to make ends meet, they appropriated and sold land, from under the farmers' noses, at throwaway prices to promoters and builders to create special economic zones, development zones, private housing estates, golf courses and sports complexes.

The one thing they did not do was to trim the local bureaucracies, as that would have required putting themselves out of work or reduce their expenditure on travel, entertainment, cars, cell phones and other badges of office. To fund their administrative and developmental expenses, they imposed a growing number of *ad hoc* and often illegal, local taxes and fees on the villagers. When the villagers protested peacefully, exercising their age-old right of Rightful Resistance, they ignored them. When they took their protest to Beijing, the local cadres intimidated and often beat them. When a courageous journalist or scholar (and these were very few) wrote about their iniquities, they filed suits against them or defamation and drove them out of their jobs and their towns. When the villagers finally massed together and came in their tractors and trailers to surround the local party office, the cadres unleashed the police and local triad gangs upon them. Very occasionally they killed a few of them.

So it is not surprising that rural unrest has grown since the mid-1990s by leaps and bounds. One index is the 10-fold rise in the number of mass protests in the country from 8,700 in 1993 to 87,000 in 2005 and the 60-fold rise in the number of participants. To

Indians, these numbers may look unimpressive, but Chinese protests cannot be compared with Indian. Indians throw stones, march to government offices or burn buses first. Chinese do so last, after they have exhausted every other means of obtaining redress.

The rise in rural unrest has seriously worried the Chinese Communist Party. While many foreign scholars believe that it does not pose a threat to the stability of the regime because the discontent is confined to 'economically marginalized groups', their view is not shared by the party leaders. President Hu Jintao's shift from Jiang Zemin's single-minded focus on growth to ensuring 'social harmony' is recognition of the urgent need to address the discount. But in the end, Hu Jintao has not gone far enough or in the right direction. Starting from his re-interpretation of Jiang Zemin's *Three Represents*, he has made it clear that the one thing that will not alter is the absolute monopoly of the Communist Party over political power. The party and the party alone will continue to monopolize all the three functions of government—legislative, judicial and executive. For the people, therefore, the local party secretary will remain God. Hu Jintao's idea of reform is to reform *the party*, not the relations between the party and the people. He has made extensive changes in its cadres, replacing the growth minded with the equity minded. But as for empowering ordinary Chinese by extending elections from the village level, where the hold of local party officials is too strong for the people to break, to the township level and creating an independent judiciary, he has dragged his feet on the first and refused to even consider the second.

All the steps he has taken to soften the edges of conflict and thereby restore social harmony have been economic. Their implied premise has been that people will feel less discontent if their incomes are raised and their lives made more secure. Hence, the abolition of the two agricultural taxes and fees, the increase in the state's purchase price for agricultural produce and various subsidies to the farmers and the increased outlays on health and education. This seems to be working. There is reasonably good evidence that the number of protests has gone down after 2005 and that the standard of living in the villages has risen. But it is difficult to make out how much of the decline in unrest has been caused by the prolonged industrial boom, the greater availability of jobs and better wages and free market prices for agricultural products, and how much of it has been caused by the abolition of taxes and fees and social security measures, adopted by the government.

The distinction is important. The benefits of the boom will not outlive it. In 2008, the most recent upswing had lasted for 7 years and could not go on for much longer. When it reverses itself it is not just jobs and wage levels that will suffer, but also the local governments' revenues, which are heavily dependent upon taxes on business. Their capacity to fund the administrative and developmental responsibilities of the townships and villages, which they have had to take over after the abolition of taxes and fees, will therefore decline. Since the bulk of these costs, incurred on education, maintenance of roads, buildings and other infrastructure pensions and health are fixed costs, a decline in local government revenues, unless made good by a further financial devolution by the centre, will force the township and village administrations to bring back the taxes and fees they were levying before in other forms. Thus, as happened during the recession from 1996 to 2001, the squeeze that recession puts on incomes will be transferred to the poorest, weakest and least organized sector of society.

The Communist Party weathered the last recession without having to make political concessions, but that does not mean that it will be able to weather the next one without doing so. The base level of peasant discontent is much higher today than it was in 1996 and the protesters are far more organized. In 1996, moreover, the peasants had known 18 years of rising prosperity. This time recession will come after at most 8 years. The present boom is far more investment driven and therefore more capital intensive than the ones of the 1980s and early 1990s. As a result, it has not generated the surge in employment that had transformed rural life and drastically brought down the level of poverty between 1981 and 1995.

The last, but possibly most important difference between 1996 and today is the absence of the cell phone and the internet then and their ubiquitous presence today. These have enabled the losers from China's state-driven development to build lateral links which have increasingly defeated the local authorities' attempt to keep discontent divided into isolated pockets. The most dramatic evidence of this was provided by the Falun Gong, when thousands of its members converged on Tiananmen square in 1999 without the government having any inkling that they were going to do so. It was their capacity to defeat the institutionalized mechanisms for the isolation and fragmentation of dissent, that frightened the central government into cracking down so ruthlessly upon the movement. All these changes ensure that if recession intensifies the predatory behaviour of local cadres, the rise in discontent will be almost instantaneous and will be much better organized.

The next half-dozen years could therefore be the crucible in which China's destiny is forged. President Hu Jintao and the senior leaders of the party in Beijing are fully aware of this and have accepted the need to make political changes that will start making the party cadres and local administrations accountable to the people. The first signs of what could be an epic change came in a statement by General Secretary Hu Jintao at the 17th Party Congress: 'We will spread the practice in which candidates for leading positions in primary party organizations are recommended both by party members and the public in an open manner and by the party organization at the next higher level, gradually extend direct election of leading members in primary party organizations to more places, and explore various ways to expand inner-party democracy at the primary level.'[1] While Hu Jintao spoke of the future, the publication of the book, by the Central Party School, within weeks of the end of the Party Congress, labelled *The Fifteen Year Assault*, outlined a programme for political reform extending over the next 15 years showing that preparations for the shift had been under way for some time.[2]

The book begins with a candid admission that, beginning in the 1990s, as market reforms have deepened, 'the interests of individuals and government departments have become increasingly integrated, with the result that corruption has followed, economic policies are distorted, and the people—particularly the poor—are increasingly unhappy'. It calls for a cautious and controlled process of reform to usher in the rule of law, a greater role for non-governmental organizations (NGOs), an acceptance of the role of religion in society and a greater role for the People's Congresses at various levels.

It devotes an entire chapter to discussing the meaning of the 'rule of law'. Its author, Wang Changjiang, re-interprets it to mean that the cadres should be accountable not only to their seniors within the party but also to the people. Noting that state power belongs to the people (according to the People's Republic of China Constitution), Wang argues that the party has got around this by resorting to a variety of stratagems that have evoked cynicism among the people and discredited the party. The most commonly used stratagem is to present to the people, for all levels of election, exactly the number of candidates (all of course drawn from the party), as the number of seats to be filled. This, he points out, has made the people ridicule the election process by wondering why the party is unable to generate more talent. Accountability to the people can be introduced, he concludes, by putting up more than one candidate per seat. *The Fifteen Year Assault* also gives a cautious nod to the idea of creating an independent judiciary.[3]

If the central leaders open up membership of township and county committees to non-party members elected by the people and establish an independent judiciary whose members do not answer to the local party secretaries but only to members of the judicial branch of the central government at the next higher level, it will have created the institutions necessary to drastically reduce predatory behaviour by party cadres. China's future will then be secure.

But the tepid reforms that have been discussed by the authors and the time frame of 15 years that they have suggested, shows that the leader's acceptance of the need for political change is still, at best, grudging. This may arise from their reluctance to acknowledge the full depth of the recession that occurred in the late 1990s and their still imperfect understanding of how the reaction of local governments to another recession could further sharpen class conflict in the country.

Apart from recognizing the urgency of the need for political reform, China's leaders also have to overcome two important psychological hurdles. The first is the fear that making even a limited concession to the demand for empowerment could become the breach in the dyke that unleashes a torrent of demands and sweeps the entire edifice of the absolutist state away. That was what had happened in Europe in 1989 and accounted for the sudden hardening of the stance taken by the Deng Xiaoping government towards the protestors at Tiananmen square. But the fear generated in the leadership by the mere prospect of making political concessions has even deeper roots in China, because it runs against the grain of the Confucian State.

From the Han dynasty onwards, the Confucian State has dealt with political unrest and dissent by reforming itself and its practice of statecraft and not by ceding power to the populace. That way led, in the opinion of its philosophers, to chaos. As Lucien Pye pointed out, the Confucian tradition does not share the Judeo–Christian faith in dialectical process and the linearity of progress. To those steeped in it, chaos is an ever-present danger that can be kept at bay only through constant vigilance, exercised by an all-powerful state.

The state must therefore be ever ready to repel external threats and meet domestic challenges. If faced with endemic discontent, it must be ready to engage in self-analysis and to reform itself. But it must not cede power to the populace to dictate what those reforms should be. This was precisely the strategy that Hu Jintao adopted when he changed the goal of the state to the creation of a 'Socially Harmonious Society'. The kind of reforms that *The Fifteen Year Assault* contemplates thus runs against the very grain of the Chinese conception of the state.

The great battle that China still has to win in order to secure its future is therefore with its own fears. These are rooted in its history and have been so completely internalized over the past two millennia that they have become a part of its collective unconsciously. It is too early to predict how quickly its leaders will overcome that fear, and whether they will even succeed in doing so. But every day that they procrastinate will only increase their fear of removing the finger from the dyke. China's future will therefore remain unsettled till it has conquered its own fear of radical change.

Notes

Chapter 1

1. Table 23 (compiled from WB—World Development Indicators).
2. The elements that need to be eliminated from the Chinese figures are 'round-tripping' of Chinese funds (export of profits by Chinese enterprises to Hong Kong, Macao and Taiwan, and their re-import as FDI to avail of tax breaks) intra-branch loans and repayments by companies, and short- and long-term loans in foreign exchange. India's definition differed from that of the IMF mainly in their exclusion of non-repatriated profits of foreign companies. This has since been corrected.
3. *Peoples' Daily*, 12 October 2006. The World Economic Forum's international competitive ranking mentioned above is taken from the same interview.

Chapter 2

1. The data for 1978 have been taken from Pei (2006). Those for 2006 come from *China Statistical Yearbook*, Table 10.1.
2. Table 18.7.
3. ASEAN6 includes the five original members of ASEAN (Indonesia, Malaysia, Philippines, Singapore and Thailand) and Brunei Darussalam. Trade between China and Vietnam (which joined ASEAN in 1995), Laos and Myanmar (1997) and Cambodia (1999) is not material and not considered further.
4. The description is that of Pei (2006).

Chapter 3

1. I am grateful to Professor Dwight Perkins for allowing me to use these data which he presented at a seminar at Harvard in October 2006.
2. The Bank therefore came up with a third explanation. Every shift of labour from a sector where its productivity is low to one in which it is higher adds to output and therefore to the GDP growth rate, without any change in the total amount of labour being used. In principle, the same is true of capital also. The World Bank had estimated that the reallocation of labour from the state sector of industry to the non-state sector had added 0.5 per cent to the annual growth rate between 1985 and 1994, while the reallocation of labour from agriculture to industry had added 1 per cent. It is assumed that these estimates also held true in 1978–84 and for 1995, and concluded that fully 1.5 per cent of the remaining 1.6 per cent was explained by factor reallocation. That left only 0.1 per cent accounted for.

Components of Growth

Components of GDP	China 1978–95	South Korea 1960–93	Japan 1960–93
TFP* at constant returns	5.1	4.5	2.5
Plus increasing returns	1.5	2.0	1.1
Plus factor reallocation	1.5	0.34	0.26
Plus inflation	1.2	—	—
Unaccounted	0.1	1.8	1.65
Official GDP growth	9.4	8.6	5.5

Note: *Total Factor Productivity.

There are, however, two weaknesses in the factor reallocation theory. The first is that its impact is suspiciously high. By the Bank's own calculations, factor reallocation contributed only 0.26 per cent to Japan's and 0.34 per cent to South Korea's growth rate between 1960 and 1993 and nothing to that of the US during the period 1950–92. While the US may be dismissed as a mature economy, and Japan as a fairly advanced industrial society where the major structural transformation had been completed by 1960, how could factor reallocation have contributed almost *five times* as much to China's growth as to South Korea's? South Korea went through exactly the same transformation as China and achieved a 0.1 per cent higher rate of per capita growth than the World Bank's revised estimate for China (6.9 per cent).

A second problem is that of distinguishing the effect of factor reallocation from that of increasing returns to scale and changes in technology. To find a quotient for the increasing returns to scale, the authors of China 2020 used a 1995 study by Kim and Lau which showed that in a sample of other Asian countries, a 1 per cent increase in all factor of production led to a 1.3 per cent increase in output. The World Bank applied this ratio to the physical increase in labour and capital in China to calculate their contribution to growth at increasing returns of scale. But in their study, Kim and Lau had related the *total* increase in output to the total increase in labour and capital. They did not relate output increase *less factor reallocation effect* to the increase in the two factors of production. Even if China experienced the same increasing returns to scale as East Asia, the factor reallocation effect should be a part of the multiplier of 1.3 applied to the physical increase in inputs to allow for increasing returns to scale. There is thus a strong possibility that the Bank has counted the same thing twice.

3. The late Professor Dong Fureng, of Beijing University, a member of the standing committee of the National Peoples' Congress and Vice-Chairman of its Financial and Economic Committee, in 1993 told the author that this problem was most pronounced in the township and village enterprises, partly because they were unable to make the adjustments, and partly because their product mix changed too rapidly for the 'comparable price' set to remain representative over a substantial period of time (see Jha 2002).

4. In his OECD study, Maddison did highlight the defects in the methods that the NBS used to collect its data. The data are unreliable because they are not collected independently by the NBS. Instead they are submitted to the NBS by the enterprises and departments after being translated into constant price estimates by a process

prescribed to them by the NBS. This methodology is of questionable accuracy and is wide open to manipulation by enterprise managers or department heads who do not want to report underperformance.

5. See also Kynge 2002.

6. In 2005, the NBS adopted a new system for collection of data. Instead of relying on self-reporting, it now sends out about 200,000 inspectors to collect the data from the enterprises. The efficacy of this system is still to be assessed (Huang 2005).

7. A telltale indicator of the NBS' continuing dependence upon the state-owned enterprises and provincial governments for the primary data is the speed with which it is able to release fresh data. The estimates of GDP for the first half of 2006 were released less than 3 weeks after the period ended on July 20. The preliminary estimates of GDP for the entire calendar year were released in 25 days on 26 January 2006. See *The Washington Post* 2006.

Chapter 4

1. Between 1993 and 2005 the number of incidents of mass protest increased from 8,700 to 87,000 and on an average six persons took part in them for every one that did so in 1993. This is dealt with in greater detail in the later chapters.

2. It is doubtful if many developing countries would meet the OECD criterion, which seems to be tailored to meet the needs of the mature industrialized countries, especially after the onset of globalization and the migration of manufacturing industry to the newly industrialized countries. India, for example, went through a severe recession between 1997 and 2003. During almost this entire period, employment in the organized sector, for which the government has reliable data, showed employment declining at an average of 1 per cent per annum. Thousands of small and medium-sized enterprises went bankrupt but the rate of growth of GDP averaged nearly 5 per cent for the 6-year period and never fell below 4 per cent.

3. *Xinhua* report datelined Beijing 8 February. Reproduced in News From China, p. 35, 17 February 1999.

4. Jianlin (1998), citing economists of the Chinese academy of Social Sciences, writes: It is widely recognized that the root cause for the low efficiency of China's economy lies in overly duplicated industrial structures and overflowing similar products, which have brought a pervasive glut relative to Household consumption demands in the domestic market.

5. Quoting the Guangdong-Hong Kong *Information Daily*, 7 July 1996.

6. This explanation was put forward by Professor Ren Ruoen, Professor of Economics at the Administration Institute of the Beijing University of Aviation and Aeronautics. Quoted by Berger (2003).

7. See, for example, Naughton (2005). He asserts that just as the decline in total energy consumption of 19 per cent of coal consumption by 29 per cent while GDP grew by 36 per cent, between 1996 and 2000 was 'preposterous', the increase in coal consumption of 18 per cent a year and of total energy consumption by 15 per cent a year between 2000 and 2004 is equally preposterous (p. 4). His logic is not easy to follow because what makes the first set of figures preposterous was the fact that GDP and energy consumption were moving in opposite directions. This

is not so in the second period. Naughton seems to believe that, having at last got a credible figure for coal consumption in 2005, the Chinese have corrected their data for coal consumption by loading the whole of the correction onto the figures for 2001–04. Why they should do that instead of smoothing out the data from 1996 onwards is not easy to understand.

Chapter 5

1. Congressional-Executive Commission on China Issues Round table, *Ownership with Chinese Characteristics: Private Property Rights and Land Reform in the PRC*. Statement of James A. Dorn, vice-President for Academic Affairs and China Specialist, The Cato Institute, 3 February 2003. Dorn outlines the most recent institutional reforms as follows:

   - Qualified foreign institutional investors will be allowed to buy equity stakes in SOEs through the A-share (local currency) stock exchanges in Shanghai and Shenzhen.
   - Strategic foreign investors will be allowed for the first time to buy the non-tradable shares of listed and unlisted SOEs.
   - Foreign joint-venture investment funds will begin operation.
   - Private commercial banks are being established in rural areas.
   - China's first civil code has been drafted, including an entire chapter dedicated to the protection of private property rights.
   - Chinas top judge, Xiao Yang, president of the Supreme People's Court, has called for safeguarding private property rights and told a national conference in Beijing: Efforts should be made to enhance awareness of the need for equal protection of all subjects in the marketplace. Farmers will have more secure land use rights as a result of the Rural Land Contracting Law adopted in August 2002.
   - Shenzhen, the first SEZ in China, is embarking on a bold political experiment, with Beijing's approval, to limit the power of the local cadres, introduce checks and balances and cultivate the rule of law.
   - A new think tank devoted to studying political reform is planned for the Central Party School in Beijing.
   - Numerous rules and regulations not in conformity with World Trade Organization norms are being scrapped and there are plans to streamline the central government's complex bureaucracy.

   All those reforms are being driven by the need to be competitive in an increasingly global economy. To attract and retain capital in the future, China will have to continue to improve its *institutional* infrastructure.
2. The term is borrowed from Paul Krugman, *Peddling Prosperity*.
3. This is all pervasive. See for instance the statement of James A. Dorn, Vice-President for Academic Affairs, and a China specialist at the Cato Institute: 'The exact scope of the private sector is difficult to calculate because private firms often wear a 'red hat' and conceal their true identity in order to gain access to state bank loans at subsidized interest rates and other government favours. A reasonable estimate is

that the private sector now accounts for about 33 per cent of GDP.' Statement made at the round table organized by the Congressional-executive Commission on China Issues, Washington, 3 February 2003.

4. Of whom 24.5 million were in manufacturing, 4.5 million in construction and 9.1 million in wholesale and retail trade.

5. It took the Asian financial crisis to jolt Beijing into changing this law and placing all bank branches under a newly formed Central Finance Work Committee (Shih 2004).

6. See note 3.

7. OECD, 'China in the World Economy', Paris: OECD, p. 183, box—The Zhucheng Experiment.

8. This is not universally accepted, least of all by the Chinese government. For a more detailed discussion of this, see Chapter 2.

9. A detailed study of the finances of 88 township enterprises in 15 counties located in two coastal provinces of China, Jiangsu and Zhejiang, that were privatized between 1993 and 1999, showed that 42 of them had been sold at prices that were below half of their base value and 31 had been sold for less than 20 per cent. The base value was calculated as the market value of all of the firm's assets, valued individually, less 93 per cent of its financial liabilities. Even after allowing for the possibility that some of these were deliberately under priced, the very large discount on the base value reflects the poor prospects of these enterprises. See (Li and Rozelle 2003: 993).

10. A large part of the decline in the number of collectives during this period can be traced to their non-viability. From 1993 to 2002, the number of collective enterprises decreased by 3.3 million from 5,156,500 to 1,885,900. In the same period of time, the number of SOEs decreased by 780,000 from 1,951,700 to 1,172,500. The number of registered private enterprises, that is enterprises in which some or all of the shares had been sold to individuals, increased by just over 2.1 million from 237,900 to 2,435,300. This was half the number of state- and township-owned enterprises that disappeared (Fewsmith, China Leadership Monitor). In one county studied by Lynette Ong, the number of township enterprises declined from 239 in 1995 to 30 in 2003 (Ong 2006: 390). The Li and Rozelle study cited in note 6 above also notes a marked acceleration of privatization activity between 1993 and 1998. Even in the limited sense of their use of the term, in which the sale of any shares to individuals caused a firm to be declared as 'privatized', township leaders privatized only 8 per cent of the firms under their control in 1993. In 1997 and 1998, when recession was at its height, this rose to 30 per cent (p. 988).

11. The serious, potentially fatal, consequences of the deepening contradiction between political autarchy and economic freedom have been powerfully outlined by Pei (2006).

12. Huang (2006b). Had the Chinese government not believed its own GDP figures for the 1990s it might not have set so ambitious a target.

13. Derived from Table 4.2, Chapter 4, with additional data for 1995–2000 from CSY 2005.

14. In 2004, China consumed 9080 Btu per $2000 of PPP-GDP against India's 4205. Energy Information Administration. Official Energy Statistics from the US government. Energy Information Annual 2004, Table E1p.

15. The structure of China's GDP is more heavily slanted towards manufacture than India's, and India's service sector accounts for marginally more of the economy than those of other countries with similar levels of income, but these differences do not come close to accounting for the immense difference in per dollar use of raw materials. See Winters and Yusuf (2006). *Dancing with Giants*.

16. Sources: For data up to 2003, Winters and Yusuf: *Dancing with Giants*, op. cit. For 2004, The Associated Press, China's imports of oil expected to have risen 10.2 per cent in 2006, 8 January 2007.

Chapter 6

1. In Chinese accounting of this period, 'Profit' equalled the excess of current revenue over the sum of the current operating cost and the capital expenditure actually incurred in maintenance and renovation. There was no set aside for depreciation.

2. The data for net profit of the SOE sector are taken from Holz and Zhu (2002). The data for the Total fixed assets are taken from World Bank: *China 2020*, op. cit., Table 34.

3. Since the banking system was entirely in the hands of the state, the four state commercial banks had no option but to comply.

4. This number is obtained by deducting the reduction in the number of large and medium-sized enterprises (1,415 or thereabout) from the reduction in number of SOEs from 74,388 in 1997 to 53,489 at the end of 2000.

5. Internal report of the State Development Planning Commission 1997, quoted by Shih (2004: 927).

6. In Indian parlance the cash reserve ratio.

7. World Bank Beijing Office, *China Update*, November 2006, p. 3.

Chapter 7

1. Among the authors are White (1998), Kelliher (1992) and Yang (1996). A very similar account is offered in Zhou (1996). Others who have recognized this development and dwelt on aspects of its consequences for China's economic policies are Olson (2000) and Nee and Peng (1994).

2. Hongye Zhang and Xiaofeng Li (Institute of Geographic Sciences and Natural Resources Research, Chinese Academy of Sciences). Although the key reform of fixing a quota of grain for delivery by the commune to the government, and leaving the use of the balance of the land to be determined by the commune, was implemented in 1979, it took the centre four more years, till 1983, to legalize the further devolution of commune targets into village and family targets, and consequently the transfer of decision-making on how to use the land, down from the commune to the family.

3. *The China Business Review*, 1 March 1997.

4. *South China Morning Post*, (Hong Kong, 2 January 1997).

5. Estimates of extra-budgetary revenues are necessarily imprecise, because of the opacity of the accounting practices followed. The OECD made a more conservative estimate of about 8–10 per cent of GDP (*China in the World Economy*, p. 638).

Chapter 8

1. The private entrepreneurs of the Communist epoch, who had been forced to live miserable and despised existences outside the protection of the communist state because they were tainted by the middle class origins of their parents.
2. The profits in 2005 were 1.134 trillion yuan, against losses of 124 billion yuan.
3. *Number of Staff and Workers in State-Owned Units at the Year-End by Sector*. The data for 2005 are not strictly comparable with those for 1995 because in 1998 the government ceased to count the 'off-post' (*xiagang*) workers as being employed. This increased the number sharply.
4. Population by sex, household registration and region (2005). The table gives the actual results of a sample survey of 1.325 per cent of the workforce. The estimated total number of migrant workers has been calculated accordingly.
5. Mo Rong. Quoted by Pei (2006).
6. Slaughter is used here metaphorically as an omnibus term to refer to all the ways in which the workers and peasants are oppressed by the cadres.
7. This would have been relatively easy in the non-state sector, where contract work was the rule, and there were no commitments of the state to its employees safeguarded by the constitution of the People's Republic of China.
8. The base value had already discounted the company's debt. It was calculated by deducting 93 per cent of current liabilities from the sale value of assets, including land, estimated separately for each asset.
9. Number of persons employed at year end in the urban and rural areas.
10. The non-payment of employees is referred to by the Bluebook on Chinese society 2004, published by the Chinese Academy of Social Sciences. See note 3 of Chapter 5.

Chapter 9

1. By then the number of such zones had gone up to over 7,000.
2. Chapter 1. A Chinese Free Lunch. Scrutinizing reform of the share-holding system.
3. Armonk and M.E. Sharpe. A shortened version of this book was published in 2006, under the title *Will the Boat Sink the Water: The Life of China's Peasants*.
4. In October 1984, the third plenary session of the Twelfth Central Committee decided to switch the emphasis in planning back to industry. In December, the same year, an All China Agricultural Work Conference held in Beijing gave the green light for levying some additional taxes on the farmers and raising the prices of agricultural inputs.
5. Chapter 6. How did the balance shift? Available in English in *The Chinese Economy*, 38(1), January to February 2005, pp. 60–86.
6. (not surprisingly, the cost of administration rose from 5.3 per cent of the national budget in 1978 to 18.6 per cent in 2002, Pei, op. cit., p. 137).
7. Chen Guidi and Wu Chuntao, Chapter 6, How did the balance shift?
8. Estimates of off-budget revenue for the period before and after 1992 are not strictly comparable because of a re-classification of revenue categories in that year, but

the jump in the share of the budget revenue in local spending is much too large not to be significant.

9. See note 3. Armonk and M.E. Sharpe, p. 45.

10. Footnote to Howard French. 2007. 'High Speed Rail Dream Took Nightmarish Turn' *International Herald Tribune* (Indian edition), Hyderabad, 9 August, p. 4.

11. Ibid., p. 49.

12. Estimates of the size of the migrant labour force vary widely because of the different definitions in use. Based on its 2001 household survey base, the Ministry of Agriculture estimated that there were 88 million rural migrants in 2001, of whom 55 per cent came from the central region and 34 per cent from the western region. Of these 88 million, nearly 90 per cent went to urban areas (including nearby townships), with 82 per cent moving to the eastern region. Most of the people who went to the east got jobs and stayed in townships and county towns; migrants who went to provincial capitals and other large metropolitan areas were less than 30 per cent of the total. However, these figures did not include construction workers in the townships, who numbered 27 million and those who came to the cities and townships as dependents of migrants, who numbered 20 million. See Huang Ping and Frank N. Pieke, China Migration Country Study. Paper presented at the Regional Conference on Migration, Development and Pro-Poor Policy Choices in Asia. The Conference was jointly organized by the Refugee and Migratory Movements Research Unit, Bangladesh, and the Department for International Development, UK, and took place on 22–24 June 2003 in Dhaka, Bangladesh. This and all other conference papers are available from the website: www.livelihoods.org.
The most comprehensive estimate was made by the 2005 national sample survey conducted by the National Bureau of Statistics, and mentioned earlier, which gave an estimate of 147.5 million.

13. The estimate is by Cook (1996).

14. *Guangdong-Hongkong Information Daily*, 28 June 1996. Quoted by He Qinliang.

15. *Jingji ribao* (*Economic Daily*), 18 June 1998. Quoted by Cai, op. cit., p. 671.

16. Quoted by Yongshun Cai (2002a).

Chapter 10

1. There were 8,700 incidents in 1993. However, this and other figures need to be treated with caution. There are varying definitions of social unrest, and Chinese officials use different ones at different times. The figures of 8,700 in 1993 and 87,000 in 2005 were compiled by the Ministry of Public Security.

2. This has been captured by Lucien and Pye (1985) in the questions they pose at the beginning of their book *Asian Power and Politics: The Cultural Dimensions of History*. 'Does the culture tend to conceive of primitive power as…something that belonged to the distant past? Or is primitive power a continuous, lurking danger, ready to surface with any faltering of established authority? Is it something that lies ahead, as society slowly becomes more degenerate and as rulers leave the way of righteousness?…In contrast to the west, traditional Asian countries have

generally not located primitive power in the distant past but have thought of it more as an ever-lurking danger in the future.'

3. Details of the recession are given in Chapter 3, and the way in which it aggravated social discontent in Chapter 5.

4. China labor yearbook, 1994–2003 Beijing: China Statistics Press, 2004. Some of the 2004 protests involved a large number of participants. For example, it was reported that 50,000 to 100,000 peasants in Sichuan Province's Hanyuan County participated in a protest in October 2004 demanding fair compensation for land use. According to Chinese official media, in 2004, Shenzhen had three major worker strikes, each including more than 2,000 strikers.

5. Xin et al. (2004). Cited by Li (2005).

6. One possibility, in the light of what followed, is that the decay of values was far more pronounced in the eastern coastal provinces such as Guangzhou and Shanghai, but since these were the seats of power within the CCP during the Jiang Zemin regime the leaders were in no position to be more specific. Sichuan was, by contrast, a not very prosperous, not very influential central province and could easily be singled out. Its only problem was that the magnitude of dereliction was unimpressive.

7. On a scale of 1 to 5 with 3 denoting no change the respondents scored 3.21 to 3.67 on political efficacy, equal treatment, judicial independence and political rights.

8. *China Daily*, December 2004. Hu visits AIDS patients in Beijing.

9. The *Peoples' Daily* online, 16 February 2005. Chinese Leaders' Spring Festival with Disadvantaged.

10. Deutsche Presse-Agentur: Chinese premier alarmed over rural unrest, calls for reforms, 20 January 2006.

11. A more detailed account is given by Naughton (2004b).

12. Details of the overheating and the policy measures adopted are given in Chapter 4.

13. Howard French, op. cit.

14. They yielded a bare 24.2 billion yuan in 2004, which was less than 1 per cent of the total tax revenues. This was in sharp contrast to the early days of the Peoples' Republic when the agricultural tax had accounted for 39 per cent of the government's revenues. See *China Statistical Yearbook* 2005, Table 8.12. See also Wu (2005).

15. By one official estimate, released by Jin Renqing, Finance Minister in the central government, total revenues had risen from 2 trillion to 3 trillion yuan in just 3 years.

16. See also 'Labour shortage threatening industrial growth', *South China Morning Post*, 26 May 2005. But the official claim of declining unrest has been questioned by some scholars and journalists. See Magnier (2006).

17. It took the first step in this direction even earlier. From 2001 it has required the county governments to pay the fees of primary school teachers (ibid.).

18. Richard McGregor, China aims to cut wealth gap with 'New Deal' for farmers.

19. Wen Jiabao honoured his commitment. In 2007 the transfers rose to 392 billion yuan, an increase of 15 per cent (Economist: Intelligence Unit Briefing: *Rural Unrest in China*, 15 March 2007).

20. Wolfe (2007). See also Queck (2007).

21. Disclosure by Chen Xiwen, director of the State Council's rural affairs office.
22. *Tasmanian Country*, 10 March 2006.
23. Kahn and Barboza (2007). The law will take effect from 2008.
24. FT Intelligence Wire: 'Trade Unions to See 8 m More Rural Migrant Workers Join in'. Business Daily update of the *Financial Times Information Service Asia*, 16 October 2006.
25. See Chapter 6.
26. It took the first step in this direction even earlier. From 2001 it has required the county governments to pay the fees of primary school teachers (ibid.).
27. Richard McGregor: China aims to cut wealth gap with 'New Deal' for farmers.
28. Chua Chin Hon: China tries to spend its way out of urban–rural problem; core issues languish while Beijing commits $68 billion to vision of 'new socialist countryside'. *The Straits Times, Singapore*, 7 March 2006. Wen Jiabao honoured his commitment. In 2007, the transfers rose to 392 billion yuan, an increase of 15 per cent (Economist: Intelligence Unit Briefing: *Rural Unrest in China*, 15 March 2007).
29. Minchin Pei, op. cit., pp. 142–43 (see also Huang 2006).
30. FT Intelligence Wire (2006), op. cit.
31. The above incidents were culled from newspaper reports by Thomas Lum, *Social Unrest in China*. US Congressional Research Service Report to Congress, 8 May 2006. Order Code RL33416.
32. Chinese official downplays police-civilian clash over polluting brewery. BBC monitoring Asia-Pacific, 30 July 2007.
33. Cody (2005: A01, Section A). See also Watts (2005a).

Chapter 11

1. Extract from the 'Full Text of Report Delivered by Hu Jintao at 17th Party Congress,' CCTV, 15 October 2007, trans. Open Source Center, CPP20071015035 002. Quoted by Joseph Fewsmith: An Upsurge in Political Reform? China Leadership Monitor No. 24, spring 2008.
2. Ibid. Zhou Yongtian, Wang Changjiang, and Wang Anling, eds., *15 nian gongjian: 2006–2020 nian ZhongguoZhengzhi tizhi gaige yanjiu baogao* [The 15-year assault: a research report on China's political reform, 2006–20] (Beijing: Zhongyang dangxiao chubanshe, 2007). The book is edited by Zhou Tianyong, the deputy head of research at the Party School, Wang Changjiang, head of the party-building section at the Central Party School, and Wang Anling, director of research in Wuxi government.
3. Ibid.

References

Arora, Vivek B. and John Norregaard. 1997. 'Intergovernmental Fiscal Relations: The Chinese System in Perspective', IMF Staff Working Paper Wp/97/129.

Bahl, Roy W. 1999. *Fiscal Policy in China—Taxation and Intergovernmental Fiscal Relations*. Burlingame, California: The 1990 Institute.

Bahl, Roy and Jorge Martinez-Vazquez. 2003. 'Fiscal Federalism and Economic Reform in China', Georgia State University Andrew Young School of Policy Studies. Working Paper 03–13, Georgia.

Bajpai, Nirupam and Nandita Dasgupta. 2004. 'FDI to China and India: The Definitional Differences', *The Hindu Business Line*, 15 May.

Bannister, Judith. 2005. 'Manufacturing Employment and Compensation in China', *The Beijing Javelin Investment Consulting Company*, Report prepared for the US Department of Labour, Bureau of Labour Statistics. Two articles based on the report can be accessed at http://www.bls.gov/opub/mlr/2005/07/art2full.pdf.

Barboza, David. 2008. 'Chinese Builders Hit the Brakes', *International Herald Tribune*, 26 November.

Baum, Richard. 1994. *Burying Mao: Chinese Politics in the Age of Deng Xiaoping*. Princeton N.J. USA: Princeton University Press.

Berger, Yakov. 2003. 'On the Fidelity of China's Economic Growth and the "Chinese Threat"', *Far Eastern Affairs. Moscow: A Russian Journal on China, Japan and the Asia-Pacific*, (1): 46–63.

Bharati, Vivek. 2006. 'China's Economic Resurgence and Flexible Coalitions', paper presented at the conference on Power Realignments in Asia: A US India Policy Dialogue, New Delhi, Organized by the Centre for Advanced Study of India, University of Pennsylvania and the Observer Research Foundation, New Delhi, December 15–17.

Cai, Jane. 2006. 'Wealth Gap Widening, Survey Reveals; Even Middle Classes Dissatisfied with Income Distribution', *South China Morning Post*, 26 December.

Cai, Yongshun. 2002a. 'Collective Ownership or Cadres' Ownership? The Non-agricultural Use of Farmland in China', *China Quarterly*, 662–80.

———. 2002b. 'The Resistance of Chinese Laid-off Workers in the Reform Period', *China Quarterly*, 170 (June).

———. 2003a. 'Cadre Ownership or Collective Ownership. The Non-agricultural Use of Farmland in China', *China Quarterly*, 175 (September): 662–80.

Cai, Yongshun. 2003b. 'Collective Ownership or Cadres' Ownership? The Non-agricultural Use of Farmland in China', *China Quarterly*, pp. 662–80.

Callick, Rowan. 2006. 'Bitter Harvest for China's Rural Majority', *The Australian*, 13 March.

Callick, Rowan. 2007. 'China's Farmers to Share Profits from Land Deals', *The Australian (Australia)*, 31 January.

Carillo-Garcia, Beatriz. 2004. 'Rural Urban Migration in China: Temporary Migrants in Search of a Permanent Settlement', *Portal*, 1 (2).

Chan, Anita and Robert A. Senser. 1997. 'China's Troubled Workers', *Foreign Affairs*, 76 (2): 104–17.

Chan, Minnie. 2007. 'Third Riot in a Month Erupts in Chongqing', *The South China Morning Post*, 6 July.

Chen, Feng. 2006. 'Privatisation and Its Discontents in Chinese Factories', *China Quarterly*, 42–60.

China Daily. 2003. 'Sun Zhigang's Brutal Killers Sentenced', *China Daily*, 10 June.

———. 2005a. 'Building Harmonious Society Top of CPC's Task', *China Daily*, 20 February.

———. 2005b. 'Township Governments Face a Role Shift', *China Daily*, 1 April.

China Daily Editorial. 2005. 'Concrete Steps for Harmonious Society', *China Daily*, 12 March.

Ching, Frank. 2005. 'The Price of Chasing Figures', *South China Morning Post*, 17 August.

Chung-Yan, Chow. 2005. 'Textile Factory Sees Migrant Labour Returning to the Land', *South China Morning Post*, 23 September.

Cody, Edward. 2005. 'In Chinese Uprisings, Peasants Find New Allies; Protesters Gain Help of Veteran Activists', *The Washington Post*, 26 November.

Cook, Sarah. 1996. *Surplus Labour and Productivity in Chinese Agriculture: Evidence from Household Survey Data*. Sussex: Institute of Development Studies.

———. 2002. 'From Rice Bowl to Safety Net: Insecurity and Social Protection during China's Transition', *Development Policy Review*, 20 (5): 615–35.

Coonan, Clifford. 2007. 'Worried Chinese President Promises to "Purify the Internet"', *The Irish Times*, 26 January.

Faison, Seth. 1999a. 'China's Cutback Surprises Boeing and Airbus', *International Herald Tribune*, 10 February.

———. 1999b. *International Herald Tribune*, 1 January.

Fewsmith, Joseph. 2002. 'Social Issues Move to Centre Stage', *China Leadership Monitor* No. 3 (Summer).

———. 2003. 'The 16th Party Congress: Implications for Understanding Chinese Politics', *China Leadership Monitor* No. 5 (Winter).

———. 2004a. 'The Third Plenary Session of the 16th Central Committee', *China Leadership Monitor* No. 9 (Winter).

Fewsmith, Joseph. 2004b. 'Continuing Pressures on Social Order', *China Leadership Monitor* No. 10 (Spring).
———. 2005a. 'CCP Launches Campaign to Maintain the Advanced Nature of Party Members', *China Leadership Monitor* No. 13.
Financial Times Editorial. 2006. 'Consuming China: The Economy Needs Less Investment and More Spending', *Financial Times Editorial*, 2 November.
Fleisher, B. M. and D. T. Yang. 2003. 'Labor Law and Regulations in China', *China Economic Review*, 14 (4): 426–33.
French, Howard W. 2006. 'Dump Trash, Add Scavengers, Mix and Get a Big Mess', The *New York Times*, 3 April.
———. 2007. 'Dream of High Speed Rail may Prove Shanghai Politician's Final Nightmare', *The International Herald Tribune*, 8 August.
Gan, X. and Li, T. 1998. 'To Control Falsification We Must Control Its Foundations', *Zhongguo Tongji (China Statistics)*, 11: 21–2.
General Administration of Customs of the People's Republic of China, 2005. *China Customs Statistics*.
Giles, John, Albert Park and Fang Cai. 2006. 'How Has Economic Restructuring Affected China's Urban Workers', *China Quarterly*, 185 (March): 1–95.
Goodman, Peter S. 2006. 'Chinese Growth Exceeds Forecasts: Rapid Rate Adds to Fear of Overheating'. *The Washington Post*, 19 July.
Gong, Ting. 1994. *The Politics of Corruption in Contemporary China*. Westport, CN: Praeger.
Guang, Lei and Lu Zheng. 2005. 'Migration as the Second Best Option. Local Power and Off Farm Employment', *The China Quarterly*, 181 (March): 22–45.
Guangming Daily. 1998. 'Statistical Fraud in China', *Guangming Ribao (Guangming Daily)*, 24 July.
———. 2004. Chapter 5: An Ancient and Burdensome Subject, *The Chinese Economy*. 38 (1): 14–59. Translated from Guidi, Chen and Wu Chuntao. 2004. 'Tianping shi zenyang qinxie de', *Zhongguo nongmin diaocha* (A Survey of Chinese Peasants), Beijing: Zhongguo wenxue chubanshe. Translated into English by Huiping Iler and Tanya Casperson.
———. 2005. 'The Life of China's Peasants, Chapter 6', *The Chinese Economy*, 38 (1): 60–88. Translation by M.E. Sharpe, Inc., from the Chinese text.
———. 2006. *Will the Boat Sink the Water: The Life of China's Peasants*. New York: Public Affairs.
Guruswamy, Mohan. 2006. 'Will India Catch up with China?', paper presented at the CASI-ORF conference Power Alignments in Asia: China, India and the United States, New Delhi, December.
Holland, Tom. 2005. 'Hu Struts Boldly into the Minefield of Energy Efficiency', *South China Morning Post*, 14 October.
Holz, Carsten A. 2006. *The Review of Income and Wealth*, 52 [1 (35)]: 85–119.

Holz, Carsten A. and Tian Zhu. 2002. 'Assessment of the Current State of China's Economic Reforms', *The Chinese Econom·* 35 (3): 71–109.

Hon, Chua Chin. 2006. 'China Tries to Spend Its Way out of Urban–Rural Problem; Core Issues Languish while Beijing Commits $68 Billion to Vision of "New Socialist Countryside"', *The Straits Times,* Singapore, 7 March.

Huang, Cary. 2005. 'Mainland's Official GDP Figures Still Questionable', *South China Morning Post,* 6 August.

———. 2006a. 'Growth Revision Sees GDP Drop in 12 Provinces; Economic Census Reveals Extent of Over-inflated Reporting', *South China Morning Post,* 13 January.

———. 2006b. 'Mainland's Progress on Goals for Energy Efficiency "Not Promising"', *South China Morning Post,* 6 August.

———. 2007. 'Economy Rebounds from Slowdown', *The South China Morning Post,* 31 March.

Huang, Cary and Jane Cai. 2007. 'Central Bank Lifts Reserve Ratio to 10.5pc; PBOC Moves to Tighten Money Supply', *South China Morning Post,* 6 April.

Huang, Yasheng and Tarun Khanna. 2003. '*Can India Overtake China?*', *Foreign Policy* (0015-7228, 137).

Huifeng, Hu. 2007. 'Arable Land Loss Nearing Danger Point, Say Officials; Shrinking Farmland Threatens Nation's Ability to Feed Itself', *The South China Morning Post,* 14 April.

Human Rights Watch. 2007. Available online at http://www.hrw.org/cam paigns/china/beijing08/sun.htm. Accessed June 28.

Hurst, William and Kevin J. O'Brien. 2002. 'China's Contentious Pensioners', *China Quarterly,* 170 (June): 345–60.

India Abroad News Service. 2006. *Top Stories: Energy Consumption by India, China to Rise.* London: *India Abroad News Service,* November 7.

International Herald Tribune. 1998. 'General Motors' China Venture at the Cross Roads', *International Herald Tribune,* 18 December.

———. 1999. 'No Letup in Economic Overhaul, China Pledges', *International Herald Tribune,* 6–7 March.

Jha, Prem Shankar. 2002. *The Perilous Road to the Market. The Political Economy of Reform in Russia, India and China.* London: Pluto Books.

Jian, Sun. 2000. *Economic History of China Volume 2.* Beijing: Beijing Peoples' Publishing House.

Jianlin, Li. 1998. 'Economy Good Despite Severe Crisis and Flood', *China Daily,* 30 December.

Kahn, Joseph. 2004. 'China Crushed Peasant Protests; Turns Three Friends into Enemies', *The New York Times,* 13 October.

———. 2006. 'Chinese Premier Says Seizing Peasants' Land Provokes Unrest', *The New York Times,* 21 January.

———. 2007. 'Harsh Birth Control Measures Fuel Violence in China', *The New York Times,* 22 May.

Kahn, Joseph and David Barboza. 2007. 'As Unrest Rises, China Broadens Workers' Rights', *The New York Times*, 30 June.

Kai, Yongshun. 2002. 'The Resistance of Chinese Laid-off Workers in the Reform Period', *China Quarterly*, 170 (June): 327–34.

Kelliher, Daniel. 1992. *Peasant Power in China*. New Haven, CT: Yale University Press.

Kennedy, John James. 2007. 'From the Tax for Fee Reform to the Abolition of the Agricultural Tax. The Impact on Township Governments in North-West China', *The China Quarterly*, 189 (March): 43–59.

Kwong, Julia. 1997. *The Political Economy of Corruption in China*. Armonk NY: M.E. Sharpe.

Kynge, James. 2002. 'Pyramid of Power behind Numbers Game', *Financial Times*, 28 February.

Lardy, Nicholas. R. 1998. 'China and the Asian Contagion', *Foreign Affairs*, July–August: 82.

———. 2006. 'The Economic Architecture of China in Southeast and Central Asia', seminar paper for the CASI-ORF Conference, New Delhi, December 15–17.

Lee, Hongbin and Scott Roselle. 2003. 'Privatising Rural China. Insider Privatization, Innovative Contracts, and the Performance of Township Enterprises', *China Quarterly*, 176: 981–1005.

Lewis, John W. and Xue Litai. 2003. 'Social Change and Political Reform in China: Meeting the Challenge of Success', *China Quarterly*, 176: 926–42.

Li, Cheng. 2004. 'Establishing Control. Cooling Shanghai Fever and Geopolitical Implications', *China Leadership Monitor* No. 12.

———. 2005. 'Hu's Policy Shift and the Tuan Pai's Coming of Age', *China Leadership Monitor* No. 15, 1–15.

———. 2006a. 'Reshufffling Four Tiers of Local Leaders; Goals and Implications', *China Leadership Monitor* No. 18.

———. 2006b. 'Think National, Blame Local: Central-Provincial Dynamics in the Hu Era', *China Leadership Monitor* No. 17.

Li, Hongbin and Scott Rozelle. 2003. 'Privatizing Rural China: Insider Privatization, Innovative Contracts and the Performance of Township Enterprises', *China Quarterly*, 176 (December): 981–1005.

Li, Yi-Min. 2002. 'Economic Institutional Change in Post-Mao China. Reflections on the Triggering', *The Chinese Economy*, 35 (3): 26–51.

Lijiang, Zhu. 2003. 'The Hukou System of the Peoples' Republic of China: A Critical Appraisal under International Standards of Movement and Residence', *Chinese Journal of International Law*, 2 (2): 519–65.

Lucien and Mary W. Pye. 1985. *Asian Power and Politics: The Cultural Dimensions of History*. Cambridge, MA: The Belknap Press of Harvard University Press.

Ma, Guonan. 2007. 'Who Pays China's Restructuring Bill?', *Asian Economic Papers*, (Winter), Massachusetts Institute of Technology, Cambridge, MA.

Macartney, Jane. 2006. 'Student Rampage Unnerves Leaders', *The Times (London)*, 26 October.

Maddison, Angus. 1998. *Chinese Economic Performance in the Long Run*, Paris: Development Centre of the OECD.

Magnier, Mark. 2006. 'The World; China Says it's Calmed Down; Government Statistics Show a 22% Decline in Incidents of Unrest this Year. Analysts, as Usual, Advise a Grain of Salt', *The Los Angeles Times*, 8 November.

McGregor, Richard. 2005. 'Economists Cast Doubt on China's GDP Data', *The Financial Times*, October.

———. 2006. 'Report Finds Pollution in China Cost 3% of Economic Output in 2004', *Financial Times, Asia Edition*, 8 September.

Monteleone, Mike. 2006. *Knocking from Within: Contemporary Social Unrest and Its Consequences for a Stable China*. Department of East Asian Languages and Civilizations, University of Chicago.

Murphy, Cait. 2006. 'Why India Will Overtake China: Despite Recent Growth Political Repression Will Keep the Asian Tiger on a Tight Leash', *Fortune*, 31 August.

Naughton, Barry. 2004a. 'An Economic Bubble? Chinese Policy Adapts to Rapidly Changing Conditions', *China Leadership Monitor* No. 9 (Winter).

———. 2004b. 'Hunkering Down: The Wen Jiabao Administration and Macroeconomic Recontrol', *China Leadership Monitor* No. 11.

———. 2005. The New Common Economic Program: The Eleventh Five Year Plan and What It Means', *China Leadership Monitor* No. 16 (Fall).

Nee, Victor and Lian Peng. 1994. 'Sleeping with the Enemy: A Dynamic Model of Declining Political Commitment in State Socialism', *Theory and Society*, 32 (2): 253–96.

Organisation for Economic Co-operation and Development (OECD). 2000. *China in the World Economy. The Domestic Challenges to Policy*, Paris: OECD.

———. 2003. *China in the World Economy: The Domestic Policy Challenges*, Paris: OECD.

Olson, Mancur. 2000. *Power and Prosperity: Outgrowing Communist and Capitalist Dictatorships*. New York: Basic Books.

Ong, Lynette. 2006. 'The Political Economy of Township Government Debt, Township Enterprises and Rural Financial Institutions in China', *China Quarterly*, June: 377–400.

Oon, Clarissa. 2007. 'China Pledged to Crack Down on Soaring Fees', *The Straits Times*, 4 January.

Park, Albert and Dewen Wang. 2006. 'Migration and Urban Poverty in China', presented at a conference on the 'Rural-Urban Gap in the PRC', organized by the Fairbank Center for East Asian Research, Harvard University, October 6–8.

Pei, Minxin. 2006. *China's Trapped Transition: The Limits of Developmental Autocracy*. Cambridge, MA: Harvard University Press.

Perry, Elizabeth J. 2001. 'Challenging the Mandate of Heaven: Popular Protest in Modern China', *Critical Asian Studies*, 33 (2): 163–80.

Peoples' Daily. 2004. 'Initial Success Achieved in State-owned Economic Restructuring', 16 November.

Pomfret, John. 1999. 'China says its Economy Expanded', *International Herald Tribune*, 1 January.

Qingyi, Wang. 2006. *Energy Conservation as Security. China Security.* China Programme, World Security Institute, Washington DC, Summer.

Qinliang, He. 2000a. 'Chapter 1: A Socialist Free Lunch', *The Chinese Economy*, 33 (3): 32–56.

———. 2000b. 'The Pitfalls of Development, Chapter 2', *The Chinese Economy*, 33, (3): 57–88. Translated from Quingliang, He. 1998. *Zhongguo de xianjing* [China's Pitfall]. Hong Kong: Mingjing chubanshe.

Queck, Tracy. 2007. 'China Unveils Landmark Law to Protect Private Property', *The Straits Times*, Singapore, 9 March.

Ramo, Joshua Cooper. 1998. 'The Shanghai Bubble', *Foreign Policy*, (Summer).

Rawski, T. 2001. 'What's Happening to China's Growth Statistics', *China Economic Review*, 12 (4): 298–302.

Rawski, Thomas and Xiao, Wei. 2001. 'Roundtable on Chinese Economic Statistics. Introduction', *China Economic Review*, 12.

Reuters. 1999. 'High Savings Rate Cuts into Chinese Economy', *International Herald Tribune*, 6–7 March.

Richards, Chris. 2004. 'Where the Reform Does not Reach the Dust will not Vanish', *The New Internationalist*, September, 371–74.

Riva, J. P., Jr. 1983. *World Petroleum Resources and Reserves: Westview Special Study.* Boulder, CO: Westview Press.

Rosenthal, Elizabeth. 1999. *New York Times*, 16–17 January.

Rowen, Henry S. 1996. 'The Short March: China's Road to Democracy', *The National Interest*, September.

Shao, Xiaomei. 2006. 'Impacts of China's Rural Land Policy and Administration on Rural Economy and Grain Production', *Review of Policy Research*, 23 (2), China Land Surveying and Planning Institute.

Shenkar, Oded. 2005. *The Chinese Century: The Rising Chinese Economy and Its Impact on the Global Economy, the Balance of Power, and Your Job.* Wharton School Publishing.

Shih, Victor. 2004. 'Dealing with Non-performing Loans: Political Constraints and Financial Policies in China', *China Quarterly*, December: 922–44.

Solinger, Dorothy J. 2003. 'State and Society in Urban China in the Wake of the 16th Party Congress', *China Quarterly*, 176 (December): 943–59.

Sterba, James P. 1993. 'A Great Leap Where?', *Wall Street Journal*, 10 December.

Sugiyama, Yoshikuni. 2007. 'China's Economy Sways the World', *Yomiuri Shimbun*, 21 March.

Sun, Yan. 2004. *Corruption and Market in Contemporary China*. Ithaca, NY: Cornell University Press.

Swamy, Subramaniam. 2000. 'Can India Catch Up with China', *Frontline*, 17(15, 22 July–4 August).

Tao, Shi Jiang. 2006. 'Unbridled Growth Dents Hopes Energy Targets Will be Met', *South China Morning Post*, 20 July.

Tiejun, Wen and Zhu Shouyin. 1996. '"Governments" Capital accumulation and the conversion of farmland into non-agricultural uses', *Guanli shijie (Management World)*, 5: 161–69.

The Economist. 2001. 'Rocking the Boat', *The Economist*, 24 November.

———. 2005. 'Survey of India and China. The Great Divide', *The Economist*, 3 March.

The Straits Times. 2001. 'Ex-Shenyang Mayor Regrets his Life of Bribes and Favours'. *The Straits Times*, Singapore, 25 December, East Asia section page A2.

The Washington Post. 2006. 'China's Gross National Product', *The Washington Post*, 26 January.

Van Der Kamp, Jake. 2005. 'Finding the Real Growth Numbers Proving a Hard Task for Beijing', *South China Morning Post*, 7 March.

Walder, Andrew G. 2007. 'Social Stability and Popular Protest in China: How Serious is the Threat', paper presented at the International Conference on Contemporary China at Hong Kong University, 5–6 January. Available online at http://www.hku.hk/china/Full_papers/Keynote1.pdf (downloaded on 20.08.2007).

Watts, Jonathan. 2004. 'Corruption Crackdown Led to Hundreds of Communist Party Suicides', *The Guardian*, 30 January.

———. 2005a. 'Mob Attacks Key Chinese Democrat: Activist Left for Dead Near Village at Centre of Fresh Wave of Unrest', *The Guardian*, 10 October.

———. 2005b. 'Sleaze Exposed as Former Minister is Jailed', *The Guardian*, 28 December.

———. 2006. 'The Big Steal', *The Guardian*, 27 May.

Wedeman, Andrew. 2004. 'The Intensification of Corruption in China', *The China Quarterly*, 180: 895–921.

Wen Tiejun and Zhu Shouyin. 1996. 'Governments' Capital Accumulation and the Conversion of Farmland into Non-agricultural Uses', *Guanli shijie (Management World)*, 5: 161–69.

Wilson, Dominic and Roopa Purushothaman. 2003. *Dreaming with BRICS: The Path to 2050*. Goldman Sachs Global Economic Paper No. 99. https//www.gs.com.

Winters, L. Alan and Shahid Yusuf. 2006. *Dancing with Giants: China, India, and the Global Economy*. Washington: World Bank and the Institute of Policy Studies.

Wolfe, Adam. 2007. 'China's Priorities on Display at the National People's Congress', *Power and Interest News Report*, 21 March.

Wong, Daniel Fu Keung, Chang Ying Li, and He Xue Song. 2007. 'Rural Migrant Workers in Urban China: Living a Marginalised Life', *International Journal of Social Welfare*, 16: 32–40.

World Bank. 1997. *China 2020: Development Challenges in the New Century*, World Bank.

———. 2004. *China Update*, November.

Wright, Tim. 2004. 'The Political Economy of Coal Mine Disasters', *China Quarterly*, 629–46.

Wu, Elaine. 2005. 'Central Government Scraps Tax on Farmers', *South China Morning Post*, 20 December.

Xin, Ru, Lu Xueyi and Li Peilin (eds). 2004. *Zhongguo shehui xingshi fenxi yu yuce* (Analysis and Forecast on China's Social Development), Beijing: Social Sciences Academic Press.

Xinhua. 1998. 'Chinese Truck, Motorcycle Production Up', *Xinhua*, 26 October.

———. 1999a. 'China Sees Stable Economic Growth', *Xinhua*, 15 June.

———. 1999b. 'News Analysis: Interest Rate Cut to Benefit Economic Growth', *Xinhua*, 10 June.

Xueqin, Jiang. 2001. 'Fighting to Organise', *Far Eastern Economic Review*, 6 September: 72–75.

Yang, Dali L. 1996. *Calamity and Reform in China: State, Rural Society, and Institutional Change since the Great Leap Famine*. Stanford, CA: Stanford University Press.

Yaohui, Zhao, 2001. Rural to Urban Migration in China: The Past and the Present. Working Paper, CCER, Beijing University, (in Chinese).

Yap, Ray. 2004. 'Can the TFR Reduce Tensions in Rural China: The Process, Progress and Limitations', *The China Quarterly*, 177: 42–70.

Yatsko, Pamela. 2000. *New Shanghai: The Rocky Rebirth of China's Legendary City*, New York: John Wiley & Sons.

Yep, Ray. 2004. 'Can the Tax-for-fee Reform Reduce Rural Tensions in China: The Process, Progress and Limitations', *The China Quarterly*, 177: 42–70.

Yusuf, Shahid, Kaoru Nabeshima and Dwight H. Perkins. 2005. *Under New Ownership: Privatizing China's State-Owned Enterprises*. Palo Alto, CA: Stanford University Press.

Zhang, L. 1999. 'Quality Problems in Regional National Income Calculations', *Zhongguo Tongji* (China Statistics), 7:12 quoted in Rawski and Xiao 2001.

Zhou, Kate Xiao. 1996. *How the Farmers Changed China: Power of the People*. *Boulder*, Colo: Westview Press.

Index

About the Author

Prem Shankar Jha has taught as a Visiting Professor at the Indian Institute of Management Calcutta. He has also been a Visiting Fellow at Nuffield College, Oxford, 1976–77; Visiting Fellow of the Centre for International Studies, Harvard University 1995, and of the Fairbank Center for East Asian Research, 2006–07. He has also been Visiting Professor at the University of Virginia (Government department) from 1997 to 2000.

Prem Shankar Jha did an MA in Philosophy, Politics and Economics from Magdalen College, Oxford, UK in 1961. After working for five years for the United Nations Development Programme, in New York, Damascus and Syria, he returned to India to pursue a career in journalism. He has been the Editor of *The Economic Times*, *The Financial Express*, and Delhi's main paper, *The Hindustan Times*. He was Economic Editor of the *Times of India* from 1981 to 1986.

In 1990, he was the Information Adviser to the Prime Minister of India, V. P. Singh. Currently, he is a columnist for *Outlook*; *The Hindustan Times*, *The Deccan Herald* and *Dainik Bhaskar* (Hindi).

He is a prolific author with many books to his right: *India: A Political Economy of Stagnation* (1980); *In the Eye of the Cyclone: The Crisis in Indian Democracy* (1993); *A Jobless Future: Political Causes of Economic Crisis (India)* (2002); *The Perilous Road to the Market: A Political Economy of Reform in Russia, India and China* (2002); *Kashmir 1947- The Origins of a Dispute* (2003). His most recent book, *The Twilight of the Nation State: Globalisation Chaos and War* was published in 2006, by Pluto Press, London, Sage Publications, India and the University of Michigan Press, Ann Arbour, Michigan, US.